'Tiger'

'Tiger'

Bill O'Reilly

60 Years of Cricket

Collins

To my best team ever–
Molly, Pat and Peter

Edited by Jack Eagan
First published by William Collins Pty Ltd, Sydney, 1985
Typeset by Midland Typesetters
Printed by The Dominion Press-Hedges & Bell

National Library of Australia
Cataloguing-in-Publication data:

O'Reilly, W.J. (William Joseph), 1905-
Tiger, an autobiography.

ISBN 0 00 217477 4.

1. O'Reilly, W.J. (William Joseph), 1905-
2. Cricket players–Australia–Biography.
3. Sportswriters–Australia–Biography. I. Title.

796.35'8'0924

CONTENTS

1 Ireland

We crossed from Northern Ireland into the Free State near Dundalk, where a team of green-uniformed excise men invaded our compartments, demanding that our bags should be opened to reveal our contraband goods, if any.

'This is a nice way,' I said, 'for an Australian cricketer to return to the land of his forefathers. Surely you don't intend to go through our luggage.'

'And what's your name, sir?' enquired the leader of the excise men.

I thought it better not to mention my Christian name, as I was well aware that William was not a highly respected name with the southerners. I just said, 'O'Reilly.'

'You wouldn't be the man who's been bowling all those Englishmen out these past few months?'

'The same,' said I.

He pulled out a stick of chalk and slashed green crosses over every bag in the compartment.

'I'm proud of you, O'Reilly. Enjoy yourself in Dublin.'

As soon as the train pulled in I was accosted by a police inspector. He took me by the arm, saying, 'Are you Bill O'Reilly?'

'I am,' I said.

'Then come along with me. We're going to a party.'

I informed the Dublin limb of the law that I had to book in

at the Shelbourne Hotel off Stephen's Green before I could contemplate my first Dublin night out.

'Give your bags to Stan McCabe,' he ordered. He had obviously done his homework.

Beaten all ends up, I conferred with Stan about my baggage and accommodation and received his smile of assent with the remark 'I wish he'd invited me too. It sounds like you're in for a good night.'

He was right. I was whisked off in a police car to the home of Dr Larry Masterson, a cousin of my wife's.

The night commenced with my introduction to Irish Whiskey, served in such lavish style that its remarkable tongue-loosening qualities emboldened me to tell my host that it had an unusual taste.

'That's the smoke of the peat,' said he.

'I've tasted only Scotch whisky before tonight.'

'Sure you'll get none of that here,' came his reply.

I was dropped, probably in a heap, at the entrance to the Shelbourne at 3 a.m. I rang the old-fashioned pull-out bell and was admitted by an ancient night porter who looked to me as though he might have become apprenticed during the days of the great patriot Daniel O'Connell. He told me he had been waiting up for me, on the instructions of my captain, McCabe, and he was quick to add that the bunch of keys he was carrying happened to include the key of the taproom. I took the hint and joined the old battler in a powerful nightcap which I knew I didn't need.

I was awakened the next morning by the noisy entry of Joe Mulholland, an enterprising young Dublin barrister, whom I had met a few hours before at Larry Masterson's home.

'Get up Bill, and shake a leg. I've brought a man along who wants to wish you good day, he's waiting down below. He has already, I am told, played a very nasty trick on you.'

Making my painful entry into the Shelbourne's loungeroom with every physical and mental response indicating that this was the morning after the night before, I was ushered into the presence of the Reverend Father Andrew Wogan, the Franciscan parish priest formerly of St Francis's Church, Paddington, New South Wales, where he had done the honours at my wedding with Molly Herbert some twelve months before.

After a very light breakfast my new-found friend Mulholland took me on one of the finest voyages of discovery I have ever experienced. First to the Dail Eireann, Ireland's Parliament, in Leinster House, Merrion Street, where he insisted that I seat myself in the Prime Ministerial chair of the celebrated Eamon de Valera.

As we left the Dail I noticed a most hideous bronze statue of HM Queen Victoria occupying the prime position in the Dail's surrounds.

Realizing that the Irish had taken great pains since 1922 to obliterate all signs suggesting they had ever been part of the Empire, I sought Joe's explanation of Her Majesty's presence.

'Take a look at it, will you?' he said. 'What do you think of it yourself?'

'I think it's ghastly,' I replied. Any part of it not covered in soot and grime seemed to have been adequately attended to by the pigeons.

'That's why we have left it there,' said Joe. 'We call it "Ireland's revenge".'

Careering at speed round the streets on either side of the Liffey River, Joe pointed out the places where such historic figures as Dean Swift, Edmund Burke, Thomas Moore, the Duke of Wellington, Oscar Wilde, George Bernard Shaw, James Joyce and Wolfe Tone were born. He spoke of each as if their luck in having been born in his beloved Dublin was more a feather in their caps than the famous accomplishments with which history has credited them.

We made a quick visit to the Brazen Head Pub on the banks of the Liffey, closely associated with the pathetic life of Robert Emmett, who at the age of twenty-five was hanged for the part he had played as a minor organizer in the 1798 rebellion. I was singled out for the honour of being escorted up the stairway to a room where stood the writing desk used by the ill-fated young hero. The fact that some twentieth century person was seeing fit to use it as a storage place for his socks and handkerchiefs detracted nothing from the respect I had gained for the man whose memory has been canonized by the Irish nation.

I was tremendously affected by Dublin, and the manner in which

Joe presented it to me. I am certain that I was beginning to detect a resurgence of my grandfather's brogue as the morning wore on. More than once I was struck with a similarity between Irish behaviour and our Australian way of life, but nowhere so powerfully as across the bar. An Irishman enters a pub on purpose bent. His approach leaves no doubt in your mind that he is there on business. He slaps his money down, takes up his glass and demolishes his Guinness with the same purposeful intent as any dyed-in-the-wool Australian you meet on the other side of the world.

With my voyage of discovery ending at the base of the monument in Dublin's main street named after Daniel O'Connell, the great statesman who stood squarely up to the power of Westminster during his life-long struggle for Home Rule, Joe Mulholland suggested that it was probably time that he landed me at Trinity College Sports Square, where Australia was to take on the cricket strength of Ireland at 11.30 a.m.

To prepare me, I suppose, for a possible disappointment at Trinity College, Joe showed me a 'par' in the *Irish Independent,* Dublin's morning newspaper, where the game had been referred to as a 'foreign fixture'. Apparently this meant that there was little likelihood of getting anything like a decent crowd, as the locals would assume it was a game against England.

But that didn't worry me. Gates did not mean much to Australian tourists those days. The equivalent of $60.00 per match was regarded by our Board members as fitting reward for the services rendered by an international cricketer. There were no bonuses if the tour made a substantial profit.

Each player was advanced £50 ($100.00) before he left Australia, to make all the necessary arrangements to keep his home working with its usual serenity. He collected a further £90 at the beginning of each of the four months spent away from home. £50 was retained by the Board, to be paid on return to Australia, as a deposit on good behaviour.

On top of this parsimonious treatment, the Board insisted that each member should sign a contract of employment with them. By today's standards the terms of those contracts were ridiculously harsh: no wife of a player was able to leave Australia during the term of the cricket tour; no player could speak to the press; no player could make public appearances, sell his autograph, or sponsor items of commerce. On it went through a litany of regulations that would be laughable in comparison with playing conditions today, except that I can remember how bitter it made some of us at the time.

We were supposed to delight in our amateur status. There was no way, in those far off days, that a successful cricketer could win himself a few extra shekels from a Man of the Match award. As for the Man of the Season – imagine the size of the garage Don Bradman would have needed to hold all the cars he would have won.

Yet the system worked. No one tried to work up a schism. Anyone who did would have disappeared from the cricket scene altogether. Some members of the Board held their positions for twenty years or more. No one had ever troubled to look at the closed court system by which they were re-elected year after year. No one at the District clubs ever dared to examine or question the jobs being done at headquarters by their own elected delegates. It was the sweetest sinecure that cricket had to offer.

All that, pardon me, in reply to the *Irish Independent's* warning that we Australians had better resign ourselves to the sight of empty benches at Trinity College Oval that morning back in 1938.

As Joe Mulholland unloaded me at the door to our dressing-room he thanked me, if you please, for a very interesting morning, before he made his way back to his rooms in the city.

I retrieved my battered old cricket bag from beneath a stack of tired-looking gear, and as I was looking for a clean flannel shirt in that faithful repository, our dressing-room door was flung open as a little old white-haired priest in rather shabby clerical gear, together with a round black hat, burst through shouting my name. He headed towards me.

'Welcome to the land of the O'Reilly's. Delighted to meet you. Me name's Mick Lacey. Where's McCabe?' And after having given Stanley a similar welcome, 'Where's Fingleton? Where's Hassett?'

He had picked out the names that left no doubts of Irish lineage, and seemed to have little interest in those that didn't, but I managed to introduce him to all the other members of our side before he dragged me out of the circle of players and stood me before one of the big glass windows which looked out on the noble grey buildings of the famous university.

'This used to be ours,' he said, 'before Queen Elizabeth's time.'

He was referring of course to the Tudor Elizabeth, 'good Queen Bess', who made war upon the Irish and took possession of Dublin in 1599.

'You are a big fellow,' he remarked, 'just the size for the job I'm going to give you.' He had heard that I'd hit a few sixes in the game at Leeds, and also at Lord's.

'You see those buildings out there surrounding the ground. You notice all those great panes of glass. Well I want you to take your bat out there today and break every bloody one of them.'

With his message delivered he turned, shook hands, and left our room as hurriedly as he had entered.

When my turn came to bat and my name went up on the makeshift scoring board, the whole congregation stood to attention and cheered me all the way to the middle.

I soon put them at their ease. Facing a bowler named Ingram, I was out first ball. Regardless, my admirers stood once again and clapped me all the way back to the pavilion. It was a reception I shall never forget. Perhaps they were stirred by the sight of the scoreboard, which now showed an '0' after my name as well as before.

I never saw Father Mick Lacey again.

2 Family Pride

My grandfather, Peter O'Reilly, arrived in Australia from Ballyconnell, County Cavan, in 1865. He landed in Sydney on the steam-assisted ship *Hornet* on 25 January, and immediately applied for employment in the local police force, then entering the third year of its existence. He had already, at the age of 23, had four years experience in the Irish constabulary. He was appointed to the foot police and spent the best part of a year patrolling the streets of Sydney which was then a healthy, vigorously expanding township of some 30,000 people.

Towards the end of his first year's work, having served the mandatory probationary period, he was appointed to the southwestern Police District with its headquarters in the Riverina town of Deniliquin. It was there that he met and married his beautiful redhead, Bridget O'Donoghue, who had migrated to Victoria in 1863, along with her sister Margaret and brothers Hubert and Patrick, all the way from Ballinasloe in County Galway.

She was 14 years old when she arrived in Australia, and she could read and write, a fact worthy of special mention. One gets lots of shocks perusing the listed personal accomplishments shown on the records of entry of migrants to Australia during the nineteenth century: reading and writing capacities are recorded, along with age, gender, religion, place of origin and port of sailing. You seldom run across an Irish migrant of that period who could neither read nor write, but strangely enough remarkably few English assisted migrants had those abilities, which makes you wonder about the strange circumstances that forced people to leave their homes forever, in the days when the English Government no longer held the right to send their convicted felons to our country.

The O'Donoghue boys took up land and started into small farming, Hubert in central western Victoria in the vicinity of Avoca, and Patrick in the Kilmore area.

The two girls found their way across the Murray River to take up jobs in the Riverina district of New South Wales, in 'domestic service' as it was genteelly described.

As an interesting matter of fact, the Riverina would belong to Victoria if the original line of demarcation had been strictly observed. When Victoria became a separated self-governing colony, immediately after the gold discoveries which had made the southern area of Australia fabulously wealthy, the legal men in England laid down the rule that a line drawn from Cape Howe through the alpine country to the source of the closest western river would mark the State boundary.

In their understandable ignorance, the line was drawn from the Cape to the source of the Murray, in the hills behind the present pretty little town of Corryong. It was substantially later that more careful surveying disclosed the fact that the source of the Murrumbidgee was much closer to Cape Howe than the source of the Murray. It was too late then: New South Wales had already fastened its hooks, but legal or not legal, many citizens of the Riverina are still very much orientated to the State of Victoria. They play Australian Rules Football, they drink Carlton beer, and they send their children to school in Melbourne.

But that's by the way. Peter O'Reilly met Bridget O'Donoghue, then 20 years of age, in the Riverina township of Deniliquin, and there they married in St Michael's Church on Saturday 20 August 1870, and set about their family life which ended with her death on 20 August 1885 at Hillston, where she lies buried.

Her death certificate shows that she died of acute gastritis, after an illness lasting only three days, but that description of her fatal complaint has always baffled me. Surely gastritis was not so lethal. I know of course about the summer diarrhoea which accounted annually for hundreds of western babies, as every country graveyard testifies. I suspect they died of dehydration. But from later personal experience I reckon that Bridget O'Reilly's complaint was probably peritonitis: the result of a burst appendix. My contest with the same opponent only a few years ago was more successful, simply because I had the immediate expert attention of the medical profession.

In Bridget's time appendectomy was not even a practised surgical operation. It became so a few years after her death, but it took an emergency operation on the Prince of Wales, son of the reigning monarch, in the 1880s to make the surgery viable and popular. My own experience, coming late in my life, gave me a vivid insight into the painful experience through which my grandmother passed, without the benefit of medical assistance.

As I stood over her graveside some eighty years later a strange feeling of embarrassment and guilt engulfed me. Here lay the Irish girl responsible for my being alive and healthy. I had travelled the world in comfort as an Australian cricketer, and later as a cricket journalist, I had visited and enjoyed the land of her birth on four different occasions, but I had never paid her the slightest attention or respect in all my life.

What a heel I was! There and then I swore that I would leave no stone unturned in making a supreme effort to learn all that there was to learn about my family. I have spent twenty years on that pleasant assignment, and I am still in the process. It has given me so much pleasure and so strongly fostered my pride in my family history that I feel it was a little more than mere chance that directed me to Hillston that summer afternoon in 1965.

My maternal grandparents, Abraham Welsh and Emma Satchell, came to Adelaide with the settlement expedition which founded that colony in 1836 under Governor Hindmarsh.

Matthew Flinders had written strongly of this southern coastline of Australia in the log of his circumnavigation of the continent in 1801, and South Australia was colonized by free settlers, under a plan promoted by the great English social reformer, Edward Gibbon Wakefield, who was also influential in the colonization of New Zealand and Canada. No convicts were to be brought to this new colony close to the mouth of the Murray River. Two classes were to be encouraged to settle there. Firstly, there must be a moneyed class to supply the capital required to buy the land from the company formed to effect the settlement, and to employ the labour supplied by the second class, the working men and women who would be invited to settle.

Abraham Welsh and Emma Satchell met there and married in 1839 at the Trinity Church of England, still standing in North Terrace, and they went to live in the bushland of Walkerville, where Abraham worked as a paling splitter close by the place where the beautiful Adelaide Oval today plays host to first-class cricketers from around the world. Both came from South Devon. Neither of them could read or write. They signed their marriage certificate with a cross.

Their son James, my grandfather, was born in Adelaide and moved with his mother Emma to Bendigo when the marriage broke up. Later, working as a cattleman on a property at Murchison in Victoria, he met a young Scottish lass named Isabel Bryde who had come to Australia with her mother and father from Edinburgh, lured by the stories of the fabulous gold strikes.

William Bryde and his wife Isabella were living in the little town of Whroo, now defunct, which was the dormitory for miners working in the Balaclava open-cut gold mine near Rushworth, when Jim Welsh married their daughter Isabel in the Presbyterian church at Rushworth in 1869.

Both of them were able to sign their marriage certificate, but they lived a wandering life. Jim Welsh became a drover. He pursued the legendary tracks of the western drovers along the Darling and the Condamine into Queensland, using Ex's Creek, now Axedale, as his home base.

Later the family moved to Wilcannia on the Darling River in New South Wales, where James was accidentally killed in 1895, in a fall from a tree which he was lopping. His death and the need for some income to help the family took Isabel and her children to White Cliffs, 62 miles away, where opal had been discovered.

Isabel started a boarding establishment to house a share of the population that had drifted in to the Cliffs from all points of the compass, all hopefully determined to strike it rich in the field.

3 White Cliffs

In case you have not heard of it, White Cliffs still occupies its lonely position on the map of New South Wales far out beyond the Darling River where the crows, so they say, fly backwards to keep the dust out of their eyes.

As the population poured into that lonely outpost the need quickly arose to make adequate education facilities available to the children who had tagged along.

The New South Wales Education Act had passed safely through the hands of Henry Parkes and the New South Wales Parliament in the early 1880s and primitive arrangements were well in hand to take education to the people. Wherever a childish quorum congregated in numbers sufficient to convince the authorities in Bridge Street, Sydney, that their pioneering genius should be exercised, a school centre was set up.

When White Cliffs' turn came for attention in the education field the city department chose a lanky young redheaded country boy, Ernest Peter O'Reilly, trained as a pupil-teacher at Hillston, a mid-western town down the Lachlan. There his father, Peter O'Reilly, the local sergeant of police, presided over a young family of eight children which he managed to hold firmly together as a strongly united, happy family group, even through the stunning aftermath of the loss of his wife Bridget who died at Hillston at the age of 35, when the eldest of her brood of eight healthy kids was fourteen, the youngest ten months.

Ernest Peter, my father, having finished his pupil-teaching apprenticeship under the highly critical eye of the Hillston Public School headmaster, received notice of his first appointment by letter late in 1895. He knew that the job facing him in White Cliffs was a task fit for a resourceful young man prepared to come to close grips with hardship.

He made his way there by coach, thanks to the service provided by an American named Cobb who brilliantly organized a network of facilities that did such a valuable job in opening up the vast inland country of Australia.

Ernest arrived and settled into his new workaday world confronted with the job not only of dispensing learning at the local citadel of knowledge but also of helping to finish the construction and the adequate furnishing of the new bush school. Making rough desks and benches was a constant occupation.

Regardless of his difficulties, the young teacher took to it like a duck to water. So well indeed that he spent thirteen wonderful years there, and the stage by then was set for the fusion of the three migrating families–Irish, English and Scottish.

He met Isabel Welsh's daughter Mina at White Cliffs, and married her in 1900. During the next thirteen years it became increasingly important that the young teacher should take the necessary steps to progress in his profession by way of the annual teachers' examinations, by means of which thousands of Australian teachers improved living conditions for their wives and families, and managed finally to enlarge the horizons of their dependents. Ernest's efforts in this direction were so spectacularly courageous, that it is impossible for me to recall them without an overwhelming sense of pride in my 'old man'.

The nearest library to White Cliffs was hundreds of miles away in some distant place like Bourke or Bathurst, which were completely beyond his orbit. Textbooks had to be purchased–I still have many of them in my possession–a cash drain which must have caused hardship with a growing family.

That however was a minor problem compared with that of getting himself from White Cliffs to Hay, 500 kilometres away as the crow flies, down on the Murrumbidgee River, to sit for his written examinations each December.

He did it on a bike.

'Bicycles are become a power . . . they have obtained the speed of a horse.' So said the London *Times* in 1878. Bicycle races were being held on the Albert Cricket Ground in Redfern, the precursor of the Sydney Cricket Ground, as early as 1867, but the craze for bicycles hit the Australian colonies in the 1890s, after Dunlop had begun to market the pneumatic tyre which made the sport viable as an enjoyable pastime.

It was in that decade that Messrs Bennet and Wood of Sydney began making the Speedwell brand of bike under licence, and marketing it enthusiastically in the colony of New South Wales.

And it was then, immediately after his appointment as teacher-in-charge of the little state school at White Cliffs, that my father, during his first holiday in Sydney, bought himself the Speedwell which later served his four sons as workhorse until 1917, and rode it all the one thousand kilometres back to his far western workaday world.

He used to speak of his long rides on the bike in exactly the same terms as his sons and grandsons are accustomed nowadays to talk about a car trip of a few hundred kilometres. He was proud to recall that his was the first bike seen in White Cliffs and he loved to describe the enthusiasm of the crowd of local inhabitants who crowded round to watch him approaching over the flat country in a cloud of dust. At first they thought the distant speck was an outsized kangaroo.

To get from White Cliffs to Hay, to take his yearly exams, it was necessary for him to make a return trip of a thousand kilometres. There were some railways functioning, but none that came anywhere near requirements. Immediately after Christmas Day, he would pack his bag and set off across those dusty western tracks. He had no companions: not many White Cliffs people were interested in going to Hay. From White Cliffs it was a hundred kilometres to Wilcannia where a beautiful bridge gave an easy crossing of the Darling. A few miles east of Wilcannia the track headed due south for Ivanhoe over a sunburnt plain fit to daunt the courage of any but the most determined travellers.

The idea was to trust entirely on the 'tanks' along the route for water. These were boreholes sunk for the artesian waters which the drovers used to keep their stock alive on the long drives between central western Victoria and the western stations of New South Wales and Queensland – the area in which Banjo Paterson ran across his famous stockman Clancy.

Pity help the traveller in those parts if he were unable to organize himself expertly enough to make intelligent use of those widely separated tanks. In that area in January there was nothing much to look forward to if he misjudged the capacity of his waterbag. Century thermometer readings on the old fahrenheit scale were the order of the day.

The track from Ivanhoe, if your knowledge of direction allowed you to pick it out from the dust, led down to the little settlement of Booligal where Ernest Peter's father, policeman Peter O'Reilly had been stationed twenty years before. Booligal's reputation was and will forever be based upon its forbidding high temperature readings. So hot was Booligal that the people of the west were known to grade the competing locations in the temperature scale in ascending order of intensity: 'Hay, Hell and Booligal.'

The run from Booligal to Hay was long and dusty and just as forbidding, but there would have been some enlivening inspiration in the knowledge that a good bath and a beer were waiting at the end of the trail.

The beer, however, just in case your mouth has begun to water, would not have been of that beautifully chilled variety with which the wayfarer is regaled in the modern advertisements. Ice production units and refrigerators were a long way into the future in those closing years of the nineteenth century.

Having settled himself comfortably at Hay, his next job was to take the examinations which were the reason for his visit. There would probably have been up to half a dozen young men and women coping with the printed papers sent out from Sydney, and they would have been supervised by the inspector himself, who was regarded as a super-mortal, holding the power of professional life or death over the examinees.

Very few teachers were trained for the job in the manner in which they are handled now in the various Teachers' Training Colleges round the country. No modern student need travel far from his or her home to enjoy the facilities provided by a training college, but in my father's day the candidate for a teaching job was chosen by the headmaster of the school in which he or she had studied. He became the virtual apprentice of the head teacher, whose job it was not only to train him in all the approved methods of imparting knowledge, but also to supervise a course of studies which ensured a thorough knowledge of English, History, Geography, Geometry, Algebra, Arithmetic and a good working knowledge of Latin and French.

In those days you could forget about a secondary education if you were a bush child lacking the support of affluent parents who could afford to send you away to a boarding school. So although my father's education had conformed with all the standards required by the Education Department, that standard was the rock bottom. It was essential that years of study be devoted to the passing of examinations designed to sift the sheep from the goats and to satisfy the requirements of the Department of Public Instruction, situated in Bridge Street, Sydney.

To judge from the textbooks which have since found their way into my library, a certain English professor named Meiklejohn would have made a fortune for himself if every young teacher in the country contributed as faithfully as my father did. Meiklejohn seems to have been an authority on everything. *The Art of Writing English*, *A new History of England and Great Britain*, along with *A New Geography on the Comparative Method* are but three which serve to outline his versatility. The cheapest of the textbooks listed above was two shillings and sixpence, which was roughly one-eighth of his weekly pay.

After the exams there was the trip back home by bike over the scorching dust track via the tanks and Booligal and Ivanhoe and Wilcannia.

It inspires me still to think of it, the incredible durability and determination. I have always been inordinately proud of Ernest Peter O'Reilly, and many times the thought of his prodigiously manly efforts were all I needed to spur me on.

He must have looked back on it all as being completely worthwhile, for he brought up a large and very happy family, won himself an honoured name in his profession, and influenced the lives and careers of hundreds of young outback Australians.

Only once in those years did the young teacher play the wag on his exam commitments, and I myself was the cause of it. On the twentieth day of December 1905, Ernest O'Reilly had an urgent appointment in White Cliffs, where his assistance was required to keep a constant supply of cooling wet hessian bags spread across the corrugated iron roof of the room in which I was born. I joined a happy family of five, more or less as a Christmas present. Probably less.

I have one clear memory of White Cliffs. I remember leaving – a coach filled with people, probably my mother and the rest of the kids – and a host of children following and waving as they scrambled for marbles which were being thrown to them in handfuls by an elderly woman passenger.

Some three-quarters of a century later I was invited to return with my wife Molly as part of the celebration of 'Back to White Cliffs Week' in September 1984.

We were magnificently looked after by Gwen Rowe, the organizer of the festivities, and a host of others including the local publican Graham Wellings and his wife Maxine, and local aviators Terry McCabe, Murray McLure and Ted Davies, who delivered us to and from Cobar.

It did my heart good to see the independence and spirit and fun they still have in that lonely outback town, which is often mentioned on weather reports as the hottest place in New South Wales, and it makes me inordinately proud when I think of the little cricket ground, cleared of gibbers, behind the local pub, with a concrete wicket and an obelisk with a brass plate which bears the legend 'The Bill O'Reilly Memorial Oval'.

4 Marengo

My father was not with us when I left White Cliffs for the first time. He had gone on beforehand to take charge of the school at Marengo in January 1908. We were heading for Sydney, where we were to remain until my father had cleared the way for us in the school residence which was to become our new home. We travelled by coach to Cobar, about 400 kilometres, where we boarded the train for Sydney, still an incredible distance away.

We took up our temporary existence in Campbell Street, Milsons Point, where the bridge now makes its northern approach to the city, in a three storeyed boarding house named 'Nalgar' run by Maude Cook, who was my father's eldest sister. 'Nalgar' has long since disappeared, of course, but from its name, which is Raglan back to front, I assume that it had been built in the 1850s or soon after and took its name from the commander of the British troops engaged in the Crimean War, who is reputed to have given the order for the Charge of the Light Brigade.

On a later visit to Sydney, staying at 'Nalgar' in the summer of 1913-14, I have a vivid recollection of an evening when I took my accustomed short stroll down Campbell Street to Brown's Pub which occupied the corner Campbell Street made with Alfred Street, a few yards north of where it started from within the tramway terminus of Milsons Point. Kirribilli is the euphonious name which now defines that area. I was 9 years old, which might tend to emphasize some kind of precocity in regard to an interest in hotels, but any later tendencies I might have shown in that direction had certainly not come to light at that tender age.

As a rather lonely country boy on holidays, living in the adult world of my Aunt Maude's boarding house, I usually strolled down to the local about 9 p.m. to meet my father and my uncle, Stephen O'Rourke, a postmaster of striking presence and delightful repartee, who would be moving out at about that time, when the cry, 'Time gentlemen please', would rise above the din of animated conversation. It was nine o'clock closing in those days, before the ubiquitous Billy Hughes, who would never have known what to do with a man-sized beer, brought about the 'early closing' of Australian hostelries. Billy closed the pubs at 6 p.m. – the time when most honest men were finishing off their day's toil and setting out on their way home. No wonder the average man bore little goodwill to the 't'othersider' who manoeuvred his way to the top of the Australian political tree.

When my two jovial relatives emerged from the floodlit bar to hail me, standing in the pale gaslight, I realized that they were accompanied by a person who looked familiar to me but one whom I could not readily name. It was Henry Lawson, whose likeness I had seen so regularly in the *Bulletin* whenever I succeeded in wresting it from under my father's eye – for him the *Bulletin* was a must, and the page on the reverse side of the red cover, where all topics of great national importance were discussed, was his bible.

My father, treating me as an important member of the quartet, introduced me so ceremoniously to the celebrated Australian that my ego jumped miles higher than the flickering gaslamp which was shining high above my head.

'Mr Lawson, this is my son Bill, who knows quite a lot about you and your poetry.'

'Bill, I want you to meet my friend Henry. You will be very proud when you are an old man that you've had this bit of good luck tonight.'

I was so proud right then that I wondered what my father meant. I had read the story of 'The Loaded Dog', and had lived every phrase of it as I tried to picture the fossicking men concerned in it. 'When your pants begin to go' had given me many a childish chuckle, and 'The Waratah and the Wattle' had long been an important part of my school recitation repertoire.

Henry looked at me with kindly piercing black eyes, said, 'It's nice to met you, Bill,' and shook my hand warmly. He knew that I had been born right out in the country he loved beyond the 'Shanty on the Rise' where he had 'tramped for years till the swag he bore seemed part of himself to him' and he acknowledged the fact by referring to us both as 'men of the west'.

On that first visit, we were only in North Sydney for two months, then off we all went to Marengo, the spelling of which I assume was taken from Napoleon's horse, although in 1917, the year we left, it was changed to the more euphonious Aboriginal-style name, Murringo. In any case, we had the happiest years of our family life there. Our horizons broadened considerably, and I first came face to face with the game of cricket. I liked it immensely.

Marengo was a splendid little community, peopled by wheat and wool farmers, many of whom had come straight from Ireland. The school had been built in 1862 on the bank of the Marengo Creek, an important tributary of the Lachlan River, which it entered close by the important town of Cowra. We far western kids took the place to our hearts. The sight of green grass and healthy high trees was new to us, and having a beautiful creek with real water in it so close to our back door was a luxury almost beyond belief.

The school was situated about half a mile from the centre of the tiny town, which was of course occupied by the pub, with the Post Office hard by. No children could possibly have led more satisfying lives than we did. We had everything that healthy kids needed, it was paradise. There was lots of room to stage our sporting contests. We built a tennis court between the schoolhouse and the road which led to Bendick Murrell, and the flat across the road at the foot of School Hill gave us a magnificent opportunity to play cricket.

As my Christmas present in 1913 Santa Claus brought me a real cricket bat with a spliced handle, the standard by which every self-respecting boy begins his discerning judgement of cricket bats.

My clearest cricket memories of that idyllic period are of my first big hit with a bat, and my first big hit with the ball. Clad still in my pyjamas, I raced out to the tennis court to shape up to the first delivery from my elder brother Jack, and I bunged it clean over the wire netting fence at the other end of the court. How my heart thumped. How my cricket stocks rose. It was a sight that I have never forgotten, the ball clearing the boundary seemingly so far away. Indeed that sight I have found to be the one that thrilled me most in all my cricket experiences. My batting ambitions have never risen to greater heights than the indulgence of sending the ball flying over the fence.

A memorable hit with the ball also stayed with me for the rest of my cricketing life. Playing in a recess match on the School Hill flat, I noticed that a big boy, a few years older than I, was prone to cock the ball up close in on the leg side a few yards from his bat. My thinking was perhaps worthy of a better fate. I stationed myself in the right place to take delivery of the chance next time it came, unmindful of what might be the outcome if the bowler sent down a short one.

The powerful swipe gave me such a painful blow on the shin that it cured me for the rest of my life of any inclination to field close to the bat. From that day onward I left that job to heroes like Sid Barnes, Jack Fingleton and Victor Richardson, who later risked their lives and limbs whilst fielding in the vital short leg position for my own bowling.

Marengo played no vital part in my cricket education, but it did give me the chance to learn to know and love the game, which is the most important lesson of them all. In fact my cricket did not blossom quickly. I am sure I had a higher regard for football then, and Marengo was really a football town. Cricket did not come naturally to Irish people who, as I found out later, regarded it more or less as a foreign game which was somewhat beneath their dignity.

Rugby Union was the game which fired the local hearts. The frequent matches with Young and Boorowa were occasions which assumed the importance of Test matches, and caught the sporting imagination of us young spectators who longed for the time when our turns would come to join in the fray. It almost broke our young hearts when the local football team enlisted en masse with the AIF in 1914.

My father had brought his Speedwell bike with us to Marengo. It was heavy framed and awkwardly geared, but it saw his kids through all the experiences of learning to ride and the wonderful feeling of mobility which enabled us to 'obtain the speed of a horse'. I had many a buster off it, but it accompanied me, or vice versa perhaps, on many a grand ride to get the family mail.

I have a very clear memory of our lunch table at the school residence one day in August 1914 when, after one such ride, I heard my father read out from the *Sydney Morning Herald*: 'England declares war on Germany'.

I recall still with great dismay the melancholy news of our casualties, printed in long lists in the *Herald* in 1916 when our footballers went into action on the Somme River, where the Allies suffered formidable losses. I read that Arthur Oakes had lost his life and realized that I never would again see that wonderful fullback who could kick goals from anywhere. That ill-fated young man, who never failed to give me a friendly wave as he rode past the school on his lively bay horse, was my first sporting idol.

In those War years at Marengo, politics first crossed my path. The name Billy Hughes became household property. As Prime Minister of Australia he sponsored the two conscription referenda aimed at giving substantial reinforcements to the already substantial numbers of young men who had joined the AIF voluntarily. Clear memories remain with me of those recruiting campaigns when the eagle eye of Charles, Lord Kitchener, frowned on everyone as he pointed his accusing finger from the poster from which sprang the words 'Your King and Country need YOU', and I can still see the eye-catching soldier dressed in his khaki uniform with feathers and shining leather bandolier, coaxing the Marengo population to join up.

One middle-aged bachelor named Bill Stewart, who lived and worked as a skilled rural worker at Templemore Station, run by the Kearins family at the Gap, offered his services to the cause. He was tough, as hard as an old Blucher boot. The recruiting sergeant, feathers and all, seemed to have some doubts about his age, and in accustomed country style asked him to open his mouth so that he could inspect his teeth. Bill opened wide, showing only where his teeth used to be. Taken aback the sergeant said, 'My God man, what do you live on?'

'On the rich lucerne flats of Templemore,' was Bill Stewart's reply.

They took him along just the same. Dentures were just beginning to become popular. I bet they never put their hands on a better soldier.

Billy Hughes's popularity sank to a zero rating when, firmly believing that his second referendum attempt would be more successful than his first, he called up all the local young men in anticipation of his election victory. Away they all went, just on harvest time, to become known as the 'Hugheseliers'. It was an unfortunate move perpetrated at the most unfortunate time. Hughes lost the election, and the boys returned home. I think that Hughes was never forgiven by the hard-working farming people.

Years later, when I had the chance to meet Billy Hughes I was amazed by his smallness. For a man who had held the highest and most responsible position in the land he was so helplessly small that it seemed quite ludicrous. Had he been a successful rider in the Melbourne Cup I would have understood, but it seemed to be laughable that such a little bloke could have carried so much political clout.

Ernest Peter, with his family growing quickly to the age when secondary education was becoming important, knew that our idyllic life at Marengo was drawing to a close.

Our family had suffered its first casualty when the second child, my brother Tom, had won a State Bursary, a scholarship which had just come into existence, and had gone off to board privately in Goulburn where he attended the State High School. Realizing that this would become a recurring calamity if he made no move to arrest it, my father applied for a move to an area closer to high school facilities.

He was appointed to Wingello, twenty miles north of Goulburn, in 1917.

5 Wingello

Wingello was just a hamlet, merely a whistle stop on the railway line, but unlike Marengo, Wingello was a cricket town.

Everyone I met at the little school was a cricket crank. They didn't know anything about football, and didn't want to. The Jeffery family, who comprised at least fifty per cent of the population, were all dedicated followers of cricket and almost to a man were skilled in the playing of it. For years they had organized the local team, taking on all comers in the southern highlands area and winning for themselves a highly respected reputation as versatile performers on the cricket field.

Most of them were engaged in the timber cutting industry. They churned out the mining props required in the south coast coal mines from the vast forests of mountain ash and messmate which covered the southern highlands. Those not engaged in that undertaking were faithful employees of the Government Railways. They were the nucleus of the fettler gangs who kept the permanent way in rattling good condition.

Their common ground was cricket, which they loved with an abiding passion. This cricket atmosphere took me quite by storm, and in no time I had become so enthusiastic about it that I had begun to read everything I could find concerning the game. The weekly descriptions of the grade game in Sydney with their beautifully listed score sheets in the *Sydney Morning Herald* became my bible, and, as I write, names come back to me of Saturday afternoon players like Austin Punch, Dan Gee, Frank Merchant, Ossie Asher and Bill McCloy, long since forgotten, but who helped in no small way to fan the cricket fire which was my total interest.

My eldest brother Jack, five years my senior, was an accomplished schoolboy athlete who could perform so well in each of the popular sports of the day that he became the idol upon whom I patterned myself and to whom I naturally looked for all the encouragement a starry-eyed boy needs. After a period of eighteen months at Goulburn High School, where Jack had distinguished himself in both cricket and football, he was given an appointment with the Agriculture Department and went to live in Sydney. Residing in North Sydney he joined the North Sydney District Cricket Club and was selected immediately in their third grade side. His departure was a devastating blow to me, but his presence was still felt and indeed his move proved to be a turning point in my cricket life. I think that this turned out to be the one critical point of my career.

Let me explain.

At the North Sydney nets one Tuesday afternoon, after work for the day had finished, Jack turned out for his usual practice session to discover that the world famous leg spinner Arthur Mailey was taking part in the local practice session at the invitation of the local committee. Jack was not lucky enough to face up to the great man. I doubt he would have had the hide to have attempted to push his frame in, he was not that type – but he did something much better as far as I was concerned. Placing himself behind the nets and concentrating single-mindedly on Mailey's approach, wrist, and direction off the pitch, he learned enough to be able to write me a long letter on his observation of the 'bosey' as we used to call it then, the 'wrong 'un' as it was more commonly known in Australia in later years.

The 'bosey' was a never-ending topic of conversation with me. Since I had first read about it in the 1920-21 season, when Mailey had rekindled interest in it in the Tests against Johnny Douglas's English touring team, the topic had enthralled me. Until Jack's letter arrived, I had never read any attempt to explain the method used to make the ball turn from the off when every tell-tale sign showed that it was a leg break. I had been prepared to accept it as some skilful sleight of hand trick in which the quickness of the hand deceived the eye, similar to the tricks I had seen used by conjurers.

Jack made it quite clear to me that Mailey's wrist seemed to go right over the top whenever the ball spun from the off side. He was sure that he recognized a movement that made the leg break action of the fingers spin the ball in clockwise fashion simply because the wrist had made a much wider movement to bring the fingers right over the top so the ball came out of the back of the bowler's hand.

That was enough for me. Within a couple of days I had taught myself the simple mechanics of changing the spin from anti-clockwise to clockwise without any readily discernible changed movement of the hand.

I did it with a tennis ball. That is the best possible instrument for a juvenile spinner to use in his routine practice sessions. It is small enough for him to wrap his hand around, it is soft enough for the fingers to be dug into it firmly, and it reacts beautifully to accentuate the action of spin.

The bosey became my most prized possession. I practised it day in, day out, winter and summer alike. The old wooden gate post at the front of our family home must have been painfully aware that my interest in cricket had taken a new 'turn'–I use the term advisedly.

All this, I hope, shows the great debt I owed to my brother Jack. He supplied the information to fire the imagination of a schoolboy and to urge him on to the important task of solving his own difficulties without the help of any outside coach. It was, as I have said, the most important occurrence of my whole cricket life.

My cricket flourished apace as a result of the Wingello influence. The first to take notice of me was 'Wattie' Jeffery. He was an accomplished right-handed batsman and could bowl lofted leg breaks accurately. He had never mastered the wrong 'un, in fact he spoke of it as if it were an official secret, kept under lock and key for the likes of Dr H V Hordern and Arthur Mailey, who were bound under national defence regulations not to disclose it lest worthless cricketers like Wattie and I should get our claws on it.

It was a red letter day for the two of us when I proudly called to him across the railway line which ran down the hill about twenty yards in front of my home. He came over to watch me roll a wrong 'un down at our gate post. His reaction was well worth seeing. His admiration knew no bounds. I'm sure he thought that the two of us – even though I was then not sixteen years old – would so dominate the Southern Tablelands Cricket Association competition that our insignificant home town, Wingello, would never again see a poor day.

When I told him that I had worked the formula out for myself after receiving instruction from Jack, whom he knew well, he implored me to share the secret and become his personal coach immediately.

But sadly Wattie never did add the wrong 'un to his repertoire. His action was so grooved and his arm so stiffened that he gave up in disgust. He finally admitted to himself that even though he could spin the delivery from his backward turn of the wrist, he had no hope at all of bowling it consistently at the stumps or of keeping it to a length. He decided instead to become one of my cheer squad, so much so that he advertised my prowess near and far, never failing to prophesy that I was a certain candidate for the Australian team.

I wish he had lived long enough to have been given the satisfaction of saying, 'I told you so'.

The first real cricket match I took part in was a fixture between the boys of our town and the young men of Tallong, the next stop on the railway line as it started on the downward grade south towards Goulburn.

Cricket gear was scarce. We had only the one bat and a rather frayed six stitcher which the men's team had generously given to us for the big occasion, but we had six stumps, all machine made with metal tips, and two sets of bails. We had not much faith in the organizing capacities of the Tallong lads.

Perhaps we carried the stumps as a bit of a skite, to show the

Tallongites that we were a team of consequence. Or perhaps they were to deal with the black snakes we met en route.

We set out on foot, not long after breakfast, carrying our gear in a tattered cricket bag, two carriers at a time, proceeding along the sleepers of the permanent way. A memory comes back to me of Walter Jeffery giving me a lesson on the general set-up of the railway track as we proceeded. He spoke of ballast, rails, plates, sleepers, expansion and contraction, so confidently that he might have taken a course in the Goulburn railway workshops. His father was a fettling ganger and my team-mate had gained his expert knowledge from him.

The seven miles walk did not worry us at all. There were no flagging feet. We were all much too excited about going into action once we had tossed the coin, and showing the opposition what we had in store for them.

The site of the game was 'Hatter's Paddock', where the Hatter family had built themselves a concrete pitch of which all the local boys made constant use. The only condition attached to the privilege was that they all must conduct themselves 'like gentlemen' at all times – a small price to pay.

My contribution to the day's fun was minimal. We batted first and I never got my hands on the ball when we went to field. My only completely lucid memory of the afternoon's programme was sitting on a log under an old mountain ash taking my turn at keeping our scorebook neat and tidy as we batted. This idyllic scene was interrupted when an incredibly large ant, known to us schoolboys as a 'Jumping Joey', dug his fangs into a soft spot high up on my right thigh. Those who have suffered the same attention from this dreaded bush marauder will no doubt accept the fact that further interest in the game for me was purely incidental. The finer details of that first match of mine have long since flown from my memory, but memory can always be relied upon to put first things first. I shall never forget the ant bite.

As a pupil at Goulburn High School, where I started my secondary education in 1918, my interest in cricket, or any sporting interest I might have had, was barely noticed. This certainly was no fault of the administration of sport there.

As a 'train boy', along with about twenty kids from down the line who joined the paper train at its various stops each morning, my day began at 7.45 a.m. We arrived in Goulburn and walked to the old High School situated diagonally across Bourke Street from the St Peter and St Paul Catholic Cathedral. At 3.30 p.m. I went straight from my classroom to the railway station, to wait for the goods train listed as No. 118–how indelibly it is imprinted in my mind–to commence a two-and-a-half-hour trip back to my Wingello home.

Those years as a train boy were by far the unhappiest years of my life. How we all stuck it out God knows. That frightful evening return trip in winter was one of excruciating pain. Imagine young healthy school children trying to remember that they must always be little gentlemen when, if they sat still, they ran a good chance of freezing to death. No wonder I was never able to sympathize fully with the agonies suffered by Charles Dickens' boys at Dotheboys Hall when I was introduced to Mr Squeers in about 1919. I reckon all us boys and girls, the girls especially, deserved high civil decorations for our courage and perseverance in surviving those dreadful train trips.

Sport was almost out of the question. We had a regular half holiday for sport on Friday afternoon, but often, with a game well underway, we train kids would all have to pack up and race off to catch the dreaded No. 118. We were looked upon as nuisances really. One could easily sense a general feeling of hostility towards the kids who roamed in late so often for morning lessons, and who were always making excuses for failing to finish homework because of sheer exhaustion. We regarded ourselves as God's frozen people.

As I was handing out the decorations for surviving that ordeal, I would reserve an extra large one for my mother. Imagine, too, her task in welcoming home four children, starving and frozen to the marrow on dark winter evenings. I reckon she was lucky that we did not take a bite out of her before she could range us all up around the table. Yet she was kind and helpful throughout that time of our ordeal, and I have no memory of her ever having lost her block with us.

Many of those train kids went on to important positions in life, which probably goes to show that a taste of real adversity never does any damage to anybody, especially children. My brother Jack, who started with the Agriculture Department, went on to the Health Department and finally became the Manager of the Gladesville Hospital. My sister Nell achieved outstanding success as a country tennis player. Brother Tom spent all his working life with the Taxation Department. Fellow train kid Phillip Davenport became a Police Magistrate, and both Selwyn Betts and Max Abbey of Towrang had distinguished careers with the Railways.

As for me, the adversity didn't do me any harm either, in fact I always feel that it put the rest of my life in a more pleasant perspective.

My break came when my father decided that the train to Goulburn plan needed softening, and that I should become a boarder at St Patrick's College, Goulburn, in 1921. There, in the care of the Christian Brothers, my life took on a different aspect.

St Pat's was founded in 1874 and had earned a splendid reputation as the second oldest Catholic College in the country. I rubbed shoulders there with boys from all over New South Wales and even from Queensland and New Guinea. Studies were of paramount importance of course, but we were given unlimited sporting opportunities, and there was never any need to hurry away to catch that dreadful train. In no time I was a member of the school's football, cricket, tennis and athletic teams.

Football, as in all schools founded by the Irish order of the Christian Brothers, took pride of place in the sporting calendar. Cricket was a game to be played to the best of one's ability in the time separating football seasons. But we cricket fanatics were well catered for: there was plenty of well kept gear jealously guarded by hot-tempered Brother Daly whose lilting accent betrayed the fact that he was fresh from the southwest of Ireland.

Amongst us there was a boy named Norman O'Connell who was easily the best batsman I had met to that time. He came from a well known Goulburn family, all gifted sportsmen, and he was the first person to really get the message home to me that it needed unrelenting concentration to master the problems that cricket presented. It has always been a matter of great concern to me that

I never heard one word about the later sporting progress of O'Connell in either football or cricket, in both of which he was one of the most outstanding schoolboy exponents I have seen. I owe him a lot. I am sure he set me on the right course so far as recognizing and handling my own cricket abilities.

In 1923, my last year at St Pat's, I won the senior cup for athletics, doing well enough to create some interest from the Sydney Athletic Club. Botany Harriers invited me, through their schoolteacher secretary Dick Corish, to join them when I won a scholarship which took me to the Sydney Teachers' College for the two years 1924 and 1925.

By that time St Pat's had absolutely rearranged my life for me. From a frustrated train boy resigned to the habit of making excuses for myself in almost all my youthful activities, St Pat's gave me the chance to face squarely up to the world and it showed me quite clearly how to get on with the happy task of living my life to the full.

The headmaster, addressed as 'president' of St Pat's in my time, was a South Australian. Taciturn and asthmatic, but a past champion handball player, James Fitzgerald gave a splendid lead to all of us in the senior section of the school. His little pep talks to the football team before we set out to do lusty battle with Goulburn High were memorable affairs. He had firmly fixed in that white head of his the unshakeable conviction that Celtic blood was particularly slow to bring to the boiling point necessary for effective football. It was a fact, he said, that Irish-Australian boys were never worth a damn in the opening stages of a football match. Their opponents could run all over them. Not until skin and hair began to fly did he think that the boys from St Pat's did themselves full justice.

I reckon I learned his lesson in this as well as any of his boys ever did. No one who knew me ever accused me of wasting time in becoming fully involved in a game of cricket. I always liked to advertise my involvement from the very moment that I was handed the ball.

In my last years at St Pat's I was lucky to come under the influence of red-haired Brother Bede Xavier Dowd, who taught

Maths and also involved himself completely in organizing our sport. Brother Dowd was a perfect school master. Sparing in his praise, quick with his temper, unstinting in his efforts to organize all his kids, and as kind and considerate as a mother. I was one of his six pall-bearers when we shouldered his coffin all the way up that steep hill to the College graveyard, where he rests with James Fitzgerald.

6 Sydney

I resented going to Sydney. The city had no charm for me. I counted myself, and still do, a lucky person to have been born and brought up in the country as a member of a large, happy family.

My scholarship to the Teachers' College granted me twenty-five shillings per week, all of which I paid in board to the establishment where I went to live in Glebe Point, within walking distance of the Teachers' College in the University grounds.

There I wasted two highly important years of my life, attending lectures which had no bearing on the realities of the teaching life, presented by lecturers who seemed to have no interest whatever in the subject they were handling or in the students who had the misfortune to be listening to them. I longed for the time when I could get myself out of the place and start trying to lead a useful life.

But if I was asked now what I got of value from my two years' training for the teaching profession, I could come up with my one truthful answer: 'Some magnificent life-long friends.' And during those two years squandered sitting at the feet of false prophets I made a modest entry into metropolitan sport.

My financial resources were so meagre that I found it necessary to concenrate solely on athletics, with Botany Harriers. Dick Corish's invitation to join his Club came with the generous offer of membership free of charge. Obviously he knew just what strains my purse could stand. I found my way out to the Sydney Sports Ground every summer Saturday afternoon to ply my wares in the events I liked best: the high jump, the hop, step and jump and the shot put.

Minor successes came my way quite regularly. I found myself listed as the State's most promising junior performer in the triple jump, and rated second to Charles Ebert, who held the State record of just under six feet one inch, in the high jump. We both used the old scissors method which meant the head went at least nine feet off the ground in clearing the bar at six feet. The rolling jump was then unknown. In the triple jump my performance, somewhere over 47 feet, had not been bettered in Australia except by Nick Winter who had won the event at the Paris Olympiad in 1924, setting a world record of over 50 feet.

Winter, by the way, was a fantastic athlete. I doubt whether he did a solid hour's training for athletics since the days when he used to jump the customers' fences delivering meat as the local butcher's delivery boy in the little town of Marrar in southwestern New South Wales. He used to wear a heavy navy blue serge overcoat over the customary blue and white silk shorts and white cotton singlet, and he was a chain-smoker. When his turn came to perform, the ground marshal would call 'A W Winter' over the megaphone, Nick would rise from his reclining position on the turf of the Sydney Sports Ground, throw his lighted cigarette onto the grass nearby, rip off his black coat and in the same movement he made to fling it aside he seemed to obtain the impulse which sent him off to the board. He always seemed to hit the board plum centre, and rose gracefully on the hop with enough height to catapult himself through the step and jump. Then, without stopping for a moment to supervise the measuring being done, he turned to hurry back and pick up his cigarette butt, inhale with obvious satisfaction, don his black coat and resume his reclining position on the turf.

I wonder what the present day coaches would have thought of him.

Corish, dynamo that he was in the art of organizing sport, was also the secretary/manager, in the most honorary manner possible, of the cricket team which David Jones Ltd's Surry Hills factory fielded in the Moore Park Saturday morning competition. How a high school teacher like Corish landed a job like that the Lord only knows, but it wasn't for the money. He invited me to join the David Jones team in a match against the Randwick-Kensington Athletic Club at Malabar, then known as 'Happy Valley', one Sunday afternoon.

Taking the field with my team-mates dressed in uniforms varying from classy flannels, running shorts, bathing costumes – neck-to-knee in those days – and just plain working clothes, I landed a job fielding in the so-called outfield, which was only about thirty yards from the stumps. Tiring of the lonely job outback, where little seemed to be happening I took the liberty of enquiring from Corish, who also carried the responsibility of captaincy, what a man must do to get his name down on the bowling list.

'Can you bowl?' he asked.

'I reckon I can stick with the standard we have shown to date,' was my reply.

He sacked one of his bowlers who, somewhat gratefully, retired to my place on the boundary as I delved into my new job. I made short work of half a dozen of the Randwick-Kensington athletes and was disappointed when there were no more left. I felt I had just got into the groove. It seemed a pity to call a halt. At the end of the day Dick had signed me up as a fully fledged member of the David Jones Moore Park Competition team. There was no paperwork involved.

They were happy days when I played Saturday morning cricket, then walked down Moore Park Road to run with Botany Harriers on the Sports Ground on Saturday afternoons. The city then had taken on a shape that appealed to me enormously. No longer was I finding time to regret the dismal fact that I had foolishly left the bush. David Jones was a really happy Club where everyone was not only keen to fraternize, but was genuinely interested and appreciative of each other's successes. I loved that team. I'm not sure that I ever got to know the real names of all of them, but a few come back in grateful remembrance: Vincent, Mahoney, Elliott, and I do wish I could remember the name of the young wicketkeeper – was it Gorman? – who did a whale of a job of taking me on concrete wickets. This young man was surely destined for high places in the wicketkeeping field. I wonder where it all went wrong.

The friends I had in that team flatly refused to accept my willingness to continue with them in the 1926-27 season after I had graduated from the Teachers' College and had begun to earn sufficient money to allow me to join a Grade club. They told me in unmistakeable terms that the man who had won the competition's bowling figures for two successive seasons had no right to be wasting his time in junior cricket. It was with great reluctance that I severed my association with them. They gave me a rousing farewell one night in a hall somewhere in Surry Hills.

Then it was that in fear and trepidation, marvelling at my own overgrown estimate of my bowling ability, I made my way unknown and uninvited to the nets at North Sydney No. 2 Oval for the first practice session of the 1926-27 season.

Grade cricket always seemed to me to be far beyond my reach. I had built an aura around it in my imagination, arising I suppose from all the reading I had done in my bush days about the outstanding performances of men who seemed to me to live in an entirely different world from mine. I'll bet there are still lots of bush boys who honestly believe that Grade cricket is surrounded by an atmosphere of excellence which must always remain foreign to them. Truthfully, I marvelled at my audacity that Saturday afternoon as I handed my name and paltry credentials to a presentable young man named Ken Waugh who took and recorded them as if I were handing in my order for delivery of the local paper. My Moore Park record made no visible impression on young Mr Waugh, just as I had feared.

There was plenty of time to take stock of what was going on and who was present. I was thrilled to find that Austin Punch was on deck and ready for action. His name was so familiar to me that I had often spoken of him and his prowess as an attacking right-hand batsman of top class as if he were one of my closest friends. Sorting him out amongst the crowd of men who fielded nonchalantly as they awaited their turns to bat or bowl, I was surprised to find that Punch was as tall as I. He really looked the part in his immaculate dress. Here was a man I thought who could put my mind at rest in less than no time. Should I be lucky enough to have a bowl at him I would soon find out whether there was likely to be any future for me in my new field.

My luck was in. Perhaps through the mystic power of alphabetical order–0 and P in close association–my name was called as a bowler simultaneously with the calling of Punch to take the bat.

It was easy to finesse my way into Punch's net, to become one of three bowlers called upon to keep him busy and to reawaken the confidence of the previous season. Slipping into action 'boots and all' as the saying goes, I imagined that I was making a satisfactory impression on the Club champion. He seemed to be taking much more care over handling me than with either of the other two bowlers having a crack at him. Quite often he would come forward defensively and play straight back to me, and more than once I forced him onto his back foot to play with extra care. Things were going so nicely for me that I felt that the changeover might not be nearly so difficult as I had thought. Grade cricket, after all, might not be too big a hurdle for me to jump.

Finally I got one to pass the outside edge of Punch's bat and hit the off stump. He was surprised, but not half as surprised as I was. I realized immediately that I had made a big impression on the man whom I knew could help me most.

After our term of action was over Punch sought me out to introduce himself, to find out my name, and to talk about my bowling He quite openly admitted that he was shocked to find that I had turned from the leg to hit the stumps. To turn at my pace, he thought, was so rare on a well prepared turf wicket that he believed I might have a fine future with the club. I was delighted with the open manner in which he extended his friendship to a lonely newcomer, and I have never forgotten it. He is still my friend.

Later that same afternoon I was thrilled to discover that I had been named as a member of the Club's Second XI to play in two games on the October long weekend which signalled the start of the Syney Grade Competition.

On the Saturday afternoon we played Petersham at North Sydney, and I was overjoyed to find that Bob Golding, the talented Maths and Sports Master whom I had met at Goulburn High School, was keeping wickets for Petersham. It was Golding who, when I was a 14-year-old boy playing for Wingello against North Goulburn, had seen me and insisted that I concentrate on spin bowling where, he was adamant, my natural talents lay, and that I should abandon any thought of being a fast bowler which might occupy my youthful mind. I have been grateful to him for the timely advice these past 65 years.

On the Monday we shaped up to Gordon, at Chatswood, where I struck perhaps the most important blow in my young cricket life. We fielded and I was handed the new ball to bowl at a right-hander named Bill Gerdes, a bank official, who was regarded highly in the competition. Getting my medium-paced leg break to grip, I hit Gerdes' wicket with one which beat him from a good length. It so obviously impressed him that I was not really surprised when the square leg fieldsman came in to report what Gerdes had said to Johnny Moyes, the incoming batsman, as he passed him at the gate.

'Watch out, Johnny, he turned that one sharply from the leg.' To which Johnny replied, 'You must have been dreaming, Bill. He couldn't have–not at that pace.'

That ball to Gerdes opened up my career in big cricket. Johnny Moyes was a top line journalist, and had played first-class cricket before World War 1 for South Australia, and later for Victoria. He was a swashbuckling batsman who gave the ball a real thump in front of the wicket.

That Moyes came within my sights so early was another example of the luck of the Irish. Several times he complimented me, and later on the same day he came to interview me about the grip I was using. He spared a few lines in his column the next week to say how much he had been impressed by the bowling of a young North Sydney Second X1 right-hander. As a result of that, I believe, I was in the North Sydney First XI the following week, and the New South Wales selection committee included me in the State Practice Squad after having played only one first grade match.

7 On Leg Spin

From the day I made my first appearance for North Sydney I seem to have stirred up plenty of interest with my unusual type of medium-paced leg spinner-cum-wrong 'un.

Now that I look back over a lifetime of involvement with cricket, it strikes me that there never have been many followers of the brand of bowling that caught my fancy. Bob Cristofani who played for St George with me and with the Australian Services side with Lindsay Hassett, showed signs of developing into a talented medium-paced bowler of the same type, but his cricket future disappeared when his career led him off to England. The only other Australian top liner who got close to it in speed and style was Jack Hill, who played for Victoria and toured England with Lindsay Hassett's 1953 Australian side. I had great hopes for Hill in that summer, and I watched him compassionately from the safety of the Press Box as he bowled his leg breaks, top spinners, and wrong 'uns, all to an extra short leg. But he never quite lived up to his promise. He had it all there without the slightest doubt, but he fell short, I regret to say it, in dedication. He just did not have that 'all in' attitude which is essential for success at the very top of any sport.

Englishman Doug Wright was another to stick to principles like my own. Most of the Australian team on the tour of England in 1938 regarded Wright as the best bowler in the country at the time. Unfortunately for him, his selectors, and English cricket executives generally, had no regard whatever for spin bowling, unless it came in from the off side.

This I have always regarded as the great paradox of English cricket. They evidently despise leg spin, yet they have always been absolute suckers for it. They have tried time and again to handicap leg spin right out of the game. Why did they think it necessary to try to destroy leg spinning in the mid-1930s by introducing the infamous lbw rule which meant that a batsman could not be given out lbw if the ball pitched outside the leg stump? Why did they introduce the 55 over new ball rule which did so much for Bradman's reputation as a captain in 1948? Why even now, when the cricket world is crying out for spin bowling, is the new ball allowed after 85 six-ball overs?

The answer is simple: the English were sick to death of leg spin, and well they might have been. They could not handle it, so they decided to destroy it. They did that with such comprehensive success that the art of leg spinning is in danger of disappearing from the game. The changed rules have been so senselessly directed towards speed and swing that no thoughtful young bowling aspirant would deem it worth his while to even think of concentrating upon leg spin, and I have heard it said that modern captains dare not use leg spinners for fear that they might lose a match in three or four overs of big hitting.

One man who gave the lie to this preposterous notion was Richie Benaud, and it is significant that he was an Australian captain of considerable reputation.

Before he assumed the captaincy, Benaud had been regarded for some years as a promising all-rounder – a brilliant field and hard-hitting lower-middle order batsman who could bowl leg spin. He went to England in 1953 and 1956 on the strength of this reputation and performed without great distinction. In 1957-58 the South Africans were bemused by the wrist spin problem posed by Benaud and Lindsay Kline, and Benaud had a good tour there, but it was not until he took over the captaincy, vacated through ill-health by Ian Craig, that he made his reputation as a bowler.

He had the privilege, unusual for a spin bowler, of being able to indulge himself a little, and as a result he became a great example of being a captain having absolute confidence in leg spin bowling. His fine record was built on that confidence.

More recently, the man who has come closest to showing what can be done with leg spin, top spin and the wrong 'un since the official clamp down was the gifted Indian Chandrasekhar, who gave Australians plenty to think about when he visited our country for the second time in 1977-78. But his was a bowling voice crying in the wilderness, so to speak.

This battle must be fought, and won, if cricket is ever going to recover the majesty it has lost as a result of the banishment.

I am quite certain that I would be very much more successful in this modern brand of cricket being played in the 1980s than I was in the 1930s. Batting has gone so far down the drain that the elementary lessons of defensive footwork have been undeniably lost. To bring Australian batting back to the heights which Victor Trumper, Charlie Macartney, Don Bradman, Alan Kippax, Stan McCabe and Lindsay Hassett had raised it to in the 'thirties, it is imperative that leg spinners come back to the field as enforcers. They, more than any other, demand footwork. Expert footwork denotes top class batting. Top class batting draws the crowds. If that sounds just a bit like a juvenile attempt to solve a geometry problem, then I am glad. I tried to shape it that way. The logic is undeniable.

This is my famous hobby horse of course, I have been putting this argument with all the force I can muster for many years – for three or four decades, in fact. But I know I am right, I know that cricket has suffered a great deal because of the discrimination against leg spin, in favour of fast bowling, and I will go on saying it for as long as I live. In the last few years I have started to think that the message might be getting through.

Just about everyone in the cricket world is tired of the sight of fast bowlers pounding in hour after hour and pitching short to batsmen who are forced to duck or play ugly defensive shots. Fast bowlers with their long runs keep the over rate low, which keeps the run rate per hour low. There is not much cricket. All that needs to be done to correct the situation is to remove the rules which discriminate against spin bowlers. If a batsman is beaten, or doesn't offer a shot, and is hit on the pad by a ball which would have hit the wicket, he is morally out. He should be out in fact, under the rules.

If the rules cease to discriminate against leg spin we will soon see the slow bowler back in his rightful place. We will see more cricket, more balls bowled per hour. We will see the delightful flowing strokeplay which is in danger of disappearing from the game. We will see the real wicketkeeping skill – the art of stumping – come back into big cricket. As an added bonus we will see the rebirth of footwork. Batsmen will have to learn to use their feet properly to counter spin bowling, and better footwork will improve their ability to play strokes against the fast bowlers.

The English administrators of the 1930s have a lot to answer for. They legislated against leg spin bowling because of the dominance of the Australian leg spinners of that time. As a result they have virtually destroyed leg spin as a force in the game, and the game is a lot the worse, the less skilful and attractive, for it.

People say that all the crowds want to see these days is 'blood and thunder' – batsmen getting hit or slogging – but I don't believe that, not for one second. It would be an awful thing for cricket to pander to some hypothetical mass lowest common denominator, as television does. I would say that I have seen more big cricket than any living Australian, with the possible exception of Alan MacGilvray. I know that crowds respond to good cricket. If the administrators, by fostering the skills of the game rather than destroying them, can provide cricket of the highest possible quality, they will have no trouble finding people to watch it.

Well there! I've got that off my chest!

In the 1983-84 Australian season Pakistan brought Abdul Qadir on tour, and thereby gave young aspiring Australian spinners a fleeting glimpse of the basic importance of spin. Sadly, Qadir failed dismally on Australian wickets. Never once did he really come to grips with his responsibilities, and I believe this meant the difference betwen victory and defeat for his country in that series.

Yet Qadir possesses every desirable trick of the spinning trade.

White Cliffs Public School, about 1900

With sister Nell, mother Mina, Mary Talty (a friend from Sydney), sister Maude, myself and brothers Jack and Tom, at Wingello

The Australian XI v South Africa, fifth Test, Melbourne, 1932. *Standing:* S.J. McCabe, J.H. Fingleton, K.E. Rigg, W.J. O'Reilly, H. Ironmonger, L.J. Nash, L.S. Darling. *Seated*: C.V. Grimmett, A.F. Kippax, W.M. Woodfull, D.G. Bradman, W.A. Oldfield

Sutcliffe bowled O'Reilly 33, second Test, Melbourne, 1933. England lost this Test by 111 runs, making only 139 in their second innings, O'Reilly 5 for 66 from 24 overs

With journalist Ray Robinson on board the *Orford* on the way to England in 1934. Note the bandaged wrist, the result of a fall on the night of the fancy dress ball, during heavy weather

Australian XI at a Scarborough Festival match, 1934. *From left:* Bradman, Oldfield, Ponsford, Ebeling, McCabe, O'Reilly, Chipperfield, Woodfull, Darling, Fleetwood-Smith, Brown

My first cap won in 1931

Goulburn High School Junior XI in 1920. I am seated next to the schoolmaster.

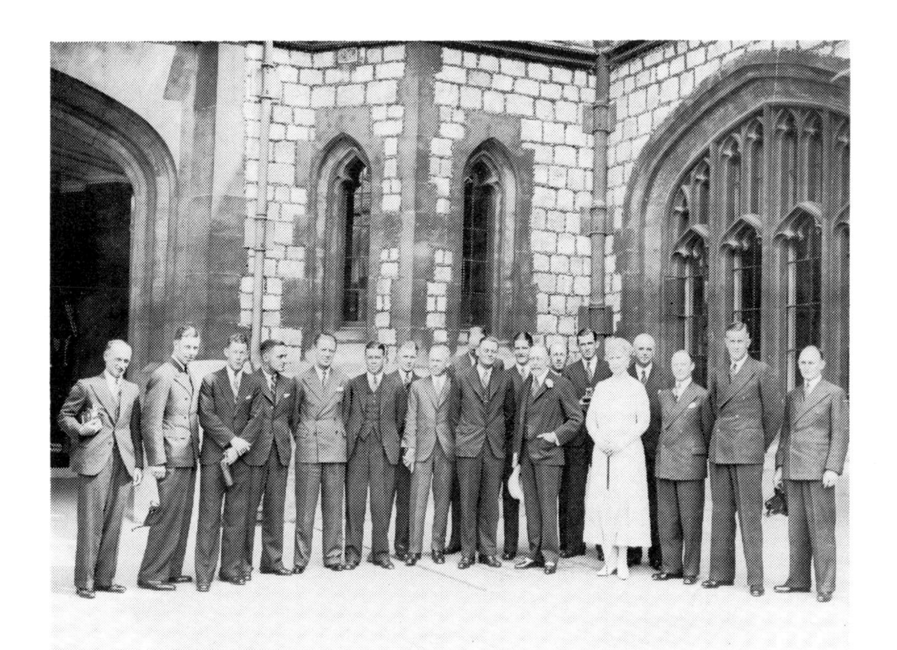

'She wore a tiny hat and leaned elegantly on a bone coloured parasol that set her off just right.' Their Majesties King George V and Queen Mary with the 1934 Australians at Windsor Castle. *From left*: Grimmett, Bromley, Brown, Darling, Kippax, Ponsford, Barnett, Bull (Treasurer), O'Reilly, Woodfull, Fleetwood-Smith, HM King George V, Chipperfield, Wall, Queen Mary, Bushby (Manager), Oldfield, Ebeling, McCabe

First day of the third Test, at Old Trafford, 1934. Hammond bowled O'Reilly, 4

Hendren caught and bowled O'Reilly, 132, at Old Trafford

Maurice Leyland caught Barnett (sub.) bowled O'Reilly after making 153 at Old Trafford. England made 627 in the first innings, but the game was drawn

His speed is just right, change of pace is well under his control, and he can spin the leg break and wrong 'un at will. What more does he need?

Two things—both of paramount importance. First, a captain capable of handling him inspiringly and of placing his field sensibly. Second, a grooved capacity to control length and direction. Each of these should have been fostered and diligently encouraged long before he reached international level. Nevertheless, he has enormous talent, and it is certainly not too late for him to make the most of it.

Towards the end of Pakistan's Australian tour in 1983-84, rumours spun around that Qadir had an ear open for an invitation to come to one of the Australian States for a season. My opinion was then, and still is, that New South Wales officials lost a great opportunity in not contracting the young Pakistani. The Sydney wicket is amenable to spin—more so than any of the other State grounds. New South Wales selectors have shown often enough that they are not afraid to select a leg spinner. Why did they not welcome the Pakistani spinner with open arms? It was a sad day for our young spinners when the chance to get Australian hands on the best spinner in modern international cricket was allowed to slip by. As Qadir perfected his own art here he would have provided the inspiration that our boys so badly need.

The first four Tests last summer, the summer of 1984-85, provided the unedifying sight of a procession of Australian batsmen mesmerized by the interminable diet of fast bowling from Garner, Marshall, Holding and Walsh. The final Test in Sydney saw the tables turned: the New South Welshmen Holland and Bennett called the tune as Greenidge, Haynes, Richardson, Richards, Gomes and Dujon prodded, propped and swayed, never knowing which way to strike. Only the cat-like Clive Lloyd was able to keep a clear head in a final Test innings of restrained pugnacity and admirable composure, as his team crumbled to an innings defeat after a record-breaking sequence without losing a Test.

Suddenly, Bob Holland was Australia's hero. Yet no one had regarded him as a world-beater before. He is indeed a very accomplished and technically competent bowler, who, like Clarrie

Grimmett, had greatness thrust upon him late in his career. He should, of course, have been recognized long ago. Only our policy of brute force – brainless speed, akin to the resurgence of violence and brutality in modern society – has kept him out of the limelight.

At least his talent has been recognized now, and the fact that he had his mate Murray Bennett bowling in tandem with him should not be ignored. Bennett is the ideal foil for Holland, spinning from the same side, but with the ability to bring his drifter – the arm ball as they call it now – in against the spin. Once Bennett had deceived Vivian Richards and removed his middle stump with a ball which drifted in against the spin, an Australian victory was assured.

Let's hope that this pair of home-grown heroes can provide the inspiration for a new generation of spin bowlers, and that our parks and back streets will no longer be filled with youngsters trying to knock their mates' heads off with juvenile bouncers, but rather using their brains and their fingers to finesse them out.

It is inspiration and example which youngsters need. Coaching has never been popular with me. I think it is good only for those boys whose interest in the game waxes and wanes so much that they are not certain whether they want to be good at it or not, who have no natural instinct for the ways and means of going about it.

A straight bat means nothing to them. Footwork is but a strange term. Length is far too obtuse. Such people need coaching. They need the attention of patient men prepared to get down to the soul-killing job of enlightenment. I feel however that talented and dedicated people should not be coached. They are the ones who are likely to become the stars. Usually they have much more innate ability than the coaches who bore them to tears with the obvious. I remember a doting parent who told me that he wanted to have his boy taught to become as good a batsman as Stan McCabe. I laughed uproariously.

There must be some good reason for having coaches I suppose. There are so many of them. But the top line player of the future can be ruined by a thoughtless coach. That type of youngster gets all that he needs out of watching a top liner in action at the nets, with the top liner completely unaware that a pair of eager youthful eyes are drinking in all the salient points about which he has been worrying so much.

Arthur Mailey, then approaching the end of his career, was watching my first appearance at the SCG nets in 1926-27, where I bowled for the first time under the gaze of the New South Wales selectors. Himself a selector, Mailey drew me aside to show me the grip he used – fundamentally different from mine – with the ball held in the fingertips of his right hand. He suggested that I should imitate it if I ever hoped to be able to spin a leg break noticeably. He went so far as to describe my own grip and to draw lines of similarity with the manner in which he himself held a golf club.

This advice appalled me. Here was a man trying to get me to dump all the lessons I had taught myself for nearly ten years. Personal lessons which I had learned well enough to find myself in attendance at the nets that afternoon.

Not likely. I thanked Mr Mailey for the great interest he had taken in me but went on to say that I thought it was much too late to be fiddling about with an action which even by that time had become second nature to me.

Looking back now I can imagine the shock that Arthur must have received. Here was a callow kid of twenty spurning advice from a proven world-beater.

I played one first-class match only with Arthur Mailey as a team-mate, and that happened to be my very first game in the Sheffield Shield Competition, in 1927. We played against Queensland on the Exhibition Ground, which ceased to be an important Brisbane cricket arena when the 'Gabba superseded it after 1928. A left-handed Queenslander named Bill Rowe batted throughout the first day for a restrained century, thereby placing his team in a position from which they took an easy victory when tropical rain gave our batsmen an impossible task when our turn came to bat.

Fielding beside Mailey in the slips late on the first day, I was brought face to face with a horrifying problem which had never previously crossed my juvenile cricket mind. Mailey took pains to warn me that I should drop any catch which might be nicked to me during the last half hour's play. Failing to understand what he was talking about, I asked him to explain himself. He did so. It was imperative, he said, that our opening batsmen should be spared the responsibilities of facing up to the new ball so late in the day, when they were worn out, and the Queensland opening bowlers fresh for the fray. The theory horrified me and I told him so.

What a thing to tell a young player! I have never forgotten that. I always think of it when I ponder over the wisdom of having professional coaches directing the destinies of young players who have made their way already into first-class teams. I wonder what Arthur Mailey would have done and said to have helped me out of the mess I would have found myself in had I 'parked a sitter'. I expect there would have been little help forthcoming.

No wonder Mailey felt inclined to use the whip on me later on when I made my way into the Australian XI. He wrote often in his column that I bowled too fast to turn the ball, and that I was certainly quite unusually lucky to gain selection over 'up in the air' spinners who got the ball to turn more sharply. He prophesied a quick return to limbo.

I admired Mailey intensely. He later became a valued friend, and in his later life we got an enormous amount of fun out of each other's company. But I never let him forget those two afternoons when he unknowingly tried to ruin my cricket career. I was lucky that all my early family training, inspired by two magnificent parents, had taught me to become wholly self-reliant. It was a great blow on my own behalf that I was able to tell him that I was prepared to sink or swim by the way I was holding the ball that afternoon back in 1926.

8 Young Don Bradman

I have often wondered about the strange fact that I still have the clearest possible recollection of the very first time I heard Don Bradman's name.

The strangeness of it comes from the present knowledge that the name must have meant absolutely nothing whatever then to a young Sydney Teachers' College student, as I was, just reaching the final stages of his two years' scholarship course and preparing to take up a job as a primary school teacher with the New South Wales Department of Public Instruction, as the Education Department was then known.

A small group of us were making our way past the 'Greasers' School', as we called Sydney University's School of Engineers, on our way down to the Forest Lodge exit from the University grounds, en route to the Jubilee Oval at Glebe Point where we were due to take part in some sporting programme. To make some sort of appropriate conversation I mentioned that I would be returning to my Wingello home where I hoped to take part in some of the cricket fixtures in the Southern Tablelands Cricket Competition during the coming two months' summer vacation. Len Kelsey, who hailed from Bowral and who had spent his two years' training at the College in close association with me, informed me that it would probably pay some dividends if I were to keep a wary eye open for a young man named Don Bradman, whom he had known as a fellow-pupil at Bowral High School, and who was presently scoring lots of runs in the local competition. I passed the matter over in the same way a good chairman in a humdrum public meeting skims over the general business, setting it aside for later consideration.

But my meeting with Bradman came much sooner than I had anticipated. Boarding a passenger train leaving Sydney's Central Station for Goulburn one Saturday morning in December 1925, I travelled peacefully for 80 miles, blithely unaware of what was to happen to me before I arrived at my little home town, situated 104 miles south. As the train came to a halt at Bowral, an attractive township popular as a health resort and holiday mountain town, I was startled out of my peaceful reverie by the weird sensation of imagining that I heard my name being called. I jumped up, leaned my long frame from the carriage window and called out 'Here I am.'

It was the stationmaster from Wingello doing the bellowing. His instructions were terse and forceful. 'Grab your bag and get out.'

My reluctance to obey him must have been plain for him to see, for he added in explanation, 'We are all down here to play Bowral this afternoon and you are going to get the new ball.' I jumped out smartly. And that was a dreadful mistake, I must admit.

The stationmaster, with the same organizing ability which had induced the Railway Commissioners to promote him to his dizzy height of responsibility, put my fears to rest by informing me that he himself had been in close contact during the week with my dear mother, who had packed my cricket gear and given it to him to set me up for the afternoon. Misguidedly I silently gave three hearty cheers for the good luck which had given me such a welcome start to the Christmas holidays.

On the way to the Bowral Oval in an old 1918 T Model Ford truck I was well and truly briefed on the growing reputation of a kid named Don Bradman—there it was again—who had been showing such unusual skill that they had decided to enlist my services at short notice.

We were a motley looking crew I suppose as we began to peel

off under cover of a clump of gum trees beside the ground. Young and old, all shapes and sizes. Moustaches were popular with the more mature members, but no youngster dared then to run the risk of wholesale criticism by encouraging the reluctant growth of a few goose-down hairs on the top lip to give the false impression that he had entered the state of manhood. It wasn't done then. There were no beards. It was long since the days when cricketers found it necessary to add to their ferocity, glamour, sex appeal—call it what you will—by hiding behind a thatch of fearsome whiskers.

Bowral won the toss and batted. I got the new ball.

You might well ask, 'Why did O'Reilly get the new ball? He wasn't a fast bowler who thrashed them down at headlong speed. There has never been any suggestion that he could move the new ball in the air sufficiently to claim recognition as a worthwhile new ball operator.'

Quite true.

O'Reilly got the new ball regardless. The reasons were basic. O'Reilly could bowl consistently at the stumps. He had earned himself a noticeable reputation as a wicket-taker in the Sydney Moore Park Saturday morning competition. Furthermore the Wingello captain and the entire team—including O'Reilly himself—thought that O'Reilly was a good bowler.

Play began.

In my first over I hit the stumps of one of Bowral's openers. That warmed me up for the entrance of a diminutive figure, approaching with what appeared to be the diffident gait of a stop-gap performer sent in to hold the fort long enough for the real number three in the batting order to get his pads on. What struck me most about him was the difficulty he seemed to be having in taking normal steps as he approached. His pads seemed to reach right up to his navel. His bat was small and had reached the sere and yellow stage, where the yellow was turning to dark tobacco.

Still, he shaped up as though he knew what the game was all about, and the expression on his face publicized the fact that he felt quite at home and was ready to cope with anything that I had in store for him.

The battle was joined. As the game proceeded I was quick to realize that I had come into contact with my very first 'problem child'. My training as a prospective primary school teacher was supposed to have prepared me for dealing with the occasional hard case who would turn up from time to time, but nothing could have prepared me for the confrontation with this particular youth.

As the precocious lad began to handle my quickish leg breaks, bouncing high off the coir mat which always favoured spin, I was made aware that here at last I had a real job of work on my hands, and I wondered what I should have to say to Len Kelsey the next time I saw him.

I had a bit of bad luck early in that memorable afternoon. Twice before he had reached 30 the youngster was dropped in the slips off my bowling. To elucidate, it is necessary that I give an honest pen-picture of the captain who led Wingello in that great struggle.

Selby Jeffery was a railway fettler. He had worn the Australian uniform which proudly displayed the big brass 'A' denoting the fact that he was present on the Sunday morning of 25 April 1915, when the Australian and New Zealand forces went into action at Gallipoli in their attempt to open up the Dardanelles. Selby was an Anzac, and as such held the unbounded respect of every man on the field. He sported a fairly robust black moustache. His face was rosy with blatant good health and his persistent good humour was heralded by the most pleasant smile one could wish to see.

His snow-white shirt and duck trousers were immaculate, as were his rubber boots. He wore a black waistcoat, unbuttoned, over the shirt. The idea of the waistcoat was quite original – it held his pipe, his tobacco and his matches. It was not unusual in those far off days for a country cricketer to light up and take a few draws on a pipe or cigarette. Nobody took umbrage at it. I saw it happen outback many times. Indeed I once saw it in first-class cricket on the Sydney Cricket Ground, when Freddie Mair, the gifted all-rounder and Balmain captain for many years, playing for New South Wales against Victoria, let his craving for a few draws get the better of him at the fall of a Victorian wicket. And I seem to recall that he had to get a match from the man fielding at short leg, but I can't remember who that was.

Selby used to slip his big-bowled bent-stemmed Captain Peterson pipe into the top pocket of his unbuttoned waistcoat. His tobacco pouch fitted snugly into the other top pocket, with the tin box holding his Wax Vestas matches in the bottom pocket along with a penknife for cutting the plug of dark 'Conqueror' tobacco.

It would have been senseless for him to field in any position where it might have been necessary to raise an occasional canter. Had he run there would have been a scattering of smoking paraphernalia in all directions. Wisely therefore he placed himself invariably at first slip where he was spendidly covered by a magnificent 'keeper named Tommy Lynam and always supported by an active and mobile second slip.

Very early in the day I got one to lift and bite. Young Bradman edged it and the ball travelled speedily and straight in the direction of Selby's midriff. It would have been an extraordinary effort had the catch been taken. It struck him in the solar plexus just at the moment when he was, with both hands well and truly occupied, lighting his pipe.

Bradman soon gave our skipper a chance to redeem himself by snicking my quicker ball straight to him again. This second time Selby made a manful attempt with both hands to make the catch, but he had blown such a dense cloud of bluish smoke from his startled lungs that he must have lost sight of the ball well before it reached him.

'Sorry Bill,' he called, as if nothing untoward had happened. Selby's inconsistencies in the slips were part and parcel of the Wingello team's programme. I was probably the only one among us who felt that he might have been wise to deny himself just a little longer.

Who in the name of all that is holy could ever possibly hope to get away unscathed when Don Bradman had been given two lives. If I said earlier that I experienced some early worries as the boyish Bradman started his innings by methodical employment of the middle of his bat, I could certainly go much further in describing my own mental reactions as this young man tore the Wingello attack apart. Even though his size suggested that he would have been better fitted physically to have been riding winners at

Randwick racecourse, he summoned up the energy required to land the ball right over the fence on half a dozen occasions. One wondered where he was hiding the battery that generated the power.

To draw a convenient veil over the desolate scene, Selby Jeffery's team finished the day a crestfallen crowd who listened more to the rattles of the old Model T Ford than to any animated flow of conversation on the thirty mile return trip by road to Wingello. Their chief bowling hope had nothing whatever to say. The boy Bradman was 234 not out.

Back at home I questioned my mother's wisdom in aiding and abetting my downfall by so carefully collecting my gear, but she seemed to think I had come to little harm, really, and that I should have considered myself lucky to have spent such a lovely day out in the fresh air playing cricket.

As the game was to be continued on our Wingello wicket the following Saturday afternoon, I could not help feeling that I was due to face up to another hammering from this pint-sized powerhouse a week later. I saw no hope ahead for me. All was gloom. I began to count my blessings in that I had other sports to choose from. As an athlete I had spent two happy years with Botany Harriers, where I had done reasonably well without ever having really tried to train assiduously for the three events – high jump, triple jump and shot put – in which I competed. I had done well enough in tennis to promise myself some sort of a future there if I cared to concentrate. All these thoughts went through my troubled boyish mind, but it was difficult to find one alleviating premise upon which to base my deep-dyed love for cricket. Having been belted unmercifully by a schoolboy was a pill too bitter for me to swallow. My pride had been badly injured.

The next Saturday afternoon arrived. I lined myself up manfully for another serve of what the game I had loved so much might have to offer.

The first ball again was mine to bowl, and the not out Bradman was there to deal with it. I let go my accustomed leg break, aimed at the leg stump. It spun sharply past the Bradman bat and crashed into the top of the off stump. Suddenly, I thought, the grass round our Wingello ground began to look greener than ever it had done before. The birds began to sing. The sun shone becomingly. One ball changed my whole sporting outlook. Gone were the dismaying plans to give the game away forever. I was prepared to go on and take whatever it had in store for me, and I made the personal pledge that as I was taking it on the chin in future I would be unsparing in my efforts to deal out as much as I could of what I was getting.

There were lots of encounters for the two of us in the years that were to follow. There were times when I felt the full weight of Don Bradman's bat – many of them indeed – but there were many occasions too when I had ample reason to rejoice in the lesson I learned on those afternoons at Bowral and Wingello in 1925.

Fifty years later I had the privilege of bowling a ball to Sir Donald Bradman when we both appeared at the ceremony to open the Sir Donald Bradman Memorial Oval built on the very site of the little park in which we met for the first time ever – long before our first-class cricket careers began.

To cap this long story off I must tell you that on 26 August 1983, the day before Don's 75th birthday, Benson & Hedges invited me to attend a function at the New South Wales Cricketers' Club in Barrack Street, Sydney, where the company presented the bat used by Bradman in the game I have described, to the NSW Cricket Association. It was the first bat he ever owned. His mammoth scores were shown thereon. That score of 234 led all the rest.

I was called upon to add a few words to the pleasant ceremony, and took the opportunity to pay a compliment or two to Sir Donald, and to his father who had so beautifully dowelled a section of willow into the edge of the bat. I am afraid that I dwelt longer than I should have on that inside edge repair job, which told of many snicked deliveries, and I claimed that many more than my actual share of these errors were committed by the maestro that memorable afternoon whilst I was bowling to him.

I was certainly not confident that I had convinced my listeners with that particular line of argument. Nor did I convince myself.

On the cricket field Bradman and I had the greatest respect for each other. I certainly did for him, and I know he did for me, but I might as well come straight out with it and let you know that, off the field, we had not much in common. You could say we did not like each other, but it would be closer to the truth to say we chose to have little to do with each other.

I don't really think that this arose from the ego-laden encounters of our younger days. It was more the product of the chemistry arising from our different backgrounds. Don Bradman was a teetotaller, ambitious, conservative and meticulous. I was outspoken and gregarious, an equally ambitious young man of Irish descent.

9 Leave Without Pay

I stand appalled, even to this day sixty years after my graduation from Sydney Teachers' College, to think that there were so many beautiful young women who trained virtually alongside me to whom I never spoke one single word. An occasional admiring stare was probably the closest I got to admitting their presence in the training struggle. Friendliness was a thing apart. What a shame that the breaking down of social barriers was not an integral part of a course aimed at preparing young men and women for their life's work in influencing the younger generation.

I can honestly say that I failed to come in contact with a staff member of the Sydney Teachers' College who could have laid any convincing claim to have been classed as a teacher in the true sense of the word.

Lecturers–yes! They were all lecturers, but that's where their claims ended. It seems to me in retrospect as I look back begrudgingly upon those two wasted years that no member of the staff could ever have had any worthwhile experience in front of a difficult class of kids clamouring for help in the job of learning.

The College principal, with a worldwide reputation as a highly acknowledged educationalist, was obviously deemed fit to see that all his 1300 students were started off on the right track. The staff surrounding him must have been chosen for some good and proper reason. If only we had known what it was.

For instance I would have deeply appreciated a simple explanation from the boss as to why it was deemed necessary to have one of his staff lecture my group for more than six months on the 'Causal Geography of the Wandering Khirghiz', an unfortunate ancient nomadic race who wandered the steppes of Central Asia and occupied such a vital status in the world's ratings that I have never heard of them since.

How often did I listen to old Griffith Taylor, a geographist of international fame who had covered his name with everlasting glory by his travels in Antarctica, come up with the conclusion that because Australia was a saucer-like shaped strip of fertile land surrounding a 'dead heart' it could never possibly support a population of twenty million people. What a theory for those of us whose fate it was to venture forth to take the torch of learning into the fertile far west of New South Wales.

These problems came forcefully into my life as soon as I found myself collecting my scattered wits when Sydney Teachers' College emptied me unceremoniously on the laps of the unfortunate children of New South Wales in 1926. Apparently I had done just enough to satisfy the examiners in a list of subjects which did little to develop my teaching techniques, and I can only presume that I was regarded as a person likely to make a good teacher if somebody should happen to take the time to tell me what the job was all about.

Fortunately for me, and for those selfsame kids, I came into immediate collision with Jeremiah Joseph Walsh, headmaster of Erskineville Primary Boys' School, where I had to learn the art of teaching with the utmost possible speed. Jerry was a man of destiny, it seemed to me. Like Goldsmith's village master at Sweet Auburn, 'a man severe he was and skilled to rule'.

In the first week under his watchful eye I learned more than had seeped through my skull in the previous two years. He taught me, metaphorically speaking, how to roll up my sleeves and hoe into the job of getting my message across to kids, and of making sure that the message was understood and likely to be remembered.

Within a month of my having first signed the time book, Jerry Walsh was well on the way towards licking me into shape. His first move was to allot me to a third class of about 40 small boys seated in a room separated from Jerry's own 6A class by a glass partition. He therefore held a strategic position from which he could observe my form through the glass as I went about my duties. I soon gathered that he was not impressed.

Holding a big blue OHMS envelope before his mouth, apparently to prevent the lads from hearing his shouted message, he would rasp out in his deep gravelly voice, 'O'Reilly! You're not worth your salt! What have I done to the Department to deserve you on my staff?' I never did find an answer for that question. Indeed I agreed with the old man entirely. I knew I wasn't worth a bumper. I would have gladly walked out. But jobs were hard to come by during those early days of the Depression.

Jerry would then go on to ask three or four kids to stand up, and with the dramatic touch of a sleight of hand entrepreneur he would say, 'Show Mr O'Reilly what you've been playing with under the desk.' Out would come the killing evidence: a comic, the core of an apple, a long piece of string, a caterpillar in the course of decapitation.

Jerry terminated each one of his frequent visits by assuring me that one day I would be glad that I started my career under his helpful attention. I doubted it. But I did find that within the course of a few months my sleuthing ability developed so acutely that I doubt one of my patients dared to bat an eyelid for fear of my holding a royal commission.

One of my summertime jobs at Erskineville was to take a tram-load of boys from the Alexandria terminus near Erskineville Station to Bent Street in the city, where we would all alight and make off to the Domain Baths at Woolloomooloo for the highly popular swimming lessons. The kids would line up on the footpath near the Mitchell Library and I would march them proudly down through the Domain. We must have been an eye-catching group. Boots and shoes were not much in evidence – many of them wore their 'everlastings' – and a patch or two on the seat of the pants was quite a feature. But I was proud of those kids and was prepared to take them anywhere that Jerry might suggest. Many of them have remained my friends for life.

One still stands out clearly in my memory as a typical, tough Australian kid, prepared to tackle any job entrusted to him. This particular lad, Albert, had a slight impediment in his speech and he was blushingly aware of it. He would start a sentence and invariably half way through there would be a blockage which caused him to shake his head up and down as though he were shaking the dregs from a bottle. All the kids loved him.

One Friday afternoon Albert's name appeared on the roster to take his turn in delivering a lecturette to the class on a subject he himself had chosen. Every boy had his turn during the year. Albert chose 'Spanish Influenza' as his topic. When he had advised me of his choice earlier in the week I was anxious about how he proposed to handle a subject that had been so terribly unpopular with Sydney people just a few years previously.

When his turn came and the class had put away their books preparing to sit back comfortably listening, I introduced him and told them what he was going to talk about. He got away to a good start with no pronounced handicap from his speech impediment, and warmed to the story of the worldwide spread of a malady that dealt a dreadful blow to mankind. Working up to his climax he told them that his own father, whom he could only just remember, had gone off to war, had spent two years without casualty in France, but coming home from it all had contracted Spanish Influenza and 'died on the bloody boat'. Realizing that the moment was almost a sacred one, not only for Albert but also for his mates, I quietly opened the door, walked out, closed it, and walked away to the staff room to give the kids a chance to recover from the unusual situation brought about by the use of the great Australian adjective in class.

Albert, when I returned to the classroom, was given a vote of thanks by one of his class-mates. It was carried by acclamation. I noticed that the clapping was much more enthusiastic than usual.

They were great kids, those 'Erko' boys. I was forever grateful that they were the ones who helped me learn from Jerry Walsh what teaching was all about.

Even now I regard teaching as a magnificent job. I never had a more satisfying one. No other job gives such instant results. A businessman must wait until he takes out his profit and loss account and writes up his balance sheet to discover how the penny has dropped for him. A teacher learns his success rating hour by hour. Imagine yourself setting out to teach a team of nine or ten-year-olds the truth about the division of fractions. You're entirely on your own. There is no sense in shouting out the rule about 'inverting the divisor and multiplying'. No matter how loudly you yell no kid has the slightest notion what you are bawling about, or what all the long words mean. But it can be done. Perhaps you will never quite get your desired 100 per cent result, but you go so close to it with coaxing, pats on the back, snarling, laughing, competitiveness, constant repetition and all the other human aids which help to motivate little children, that you can go home at the end of the day congratulating yourself on a job well done.

There was a time at Erskineville when old Jerry coaxed me into taking both the school cricket team and the Australian Rules football team all round the metropolitan area in competitions organized by the Public Schools' Amateur Athletic Association, the 'PS and three As' as it was popularly known. Once a week the *Sydney Morning Herald* found space to devote to short summaries of the week's sporting results, supplied by Bunny Gordon and Steve Lynch, two teachers who had been permanently seconded to the PSAAA office in Bridge Street, and who did a splendid job for which they got very little acknowledgment. The Department was never noted for its friendly attitude towards sport. It always seemed to me that the men who got to the top of it and thereby called the tune had never experienced the thrill of scoring a try or hitting a six in their lives.

But Jerry was deeply interested. He read out the scores every Monday morning and made a big point of bringing out any boy who had performed with distinction, and shaking his hand heartily as he praised him in front of the school lined in their ranks at the start of a week. As the young hero squirmed in agony in Jerry's grip, I often wondered whether he thought it was all worthwhile.

Jerry Walsh and I eventually developed an abiding friendship. He had cricket in his blood, but it took me a long time to realize that fact. He was an enigma to me. To meet him away from the school he was a personable companion prepared to discuss any subject, especially if it had anything to do with cricket. He thrilled over my rise in the sport. He followed me about the Sydney Grade grounds, and to Melbourne quite often in later years, and I am sure he thought that his training methods had as much to do with my success on the cricket field as they did in the classroom. Perhaps they did.

He taught me without the slightest doubt that the one important essence of teaching is the ability to attain and maintain discipline. I was always grateful to Jerry for that, but not grateful enough to accompany him to his next school when he was promoted to first-class status at Burwood. I took it as an honour that he asked me to go along, but I thought that some other young teacher was in more need of his expert attention at that stage than I.

Having successfully withstood the frightening problem presented by Jerry, no other boss gave me the least bit of worry in the fifteen happy years I spent in the profession.

It was at Erskineville that cricket first began to poke its interesting nose into my career. Not long after I had joined up with the North Sydney Grade club I was invited at short notice to play at the Sydney Cricket Ground in a Testimonial match for a young man named Proud who had been blinded in the course of a match somewhere in the Illawarra area. Public service regulations allowed the State's employees the right to apply for unpaid leave to represent their State in sport, so long as they made application for it seven days in advance. There was no chance of my taking part in the game as I could not give the required notice, although I would have dearly loved to play: it was my very first chance of mixing in with some of the great names of the game.

I informed the Cricket Association with a sinking heart that I was unavailable. Imagine then my surprise when I received a telegram addressed to me at Erskineville Public School on the morning of the match saying, 'Proceed to Sydney Cricket Ground to play in Proud Testimonial Match this afternoon'. It was signed by Sammy Lasker, the Chief Inspector of Schools, a diminutive man who carried such professional clout that one almost sprang respectfully to attention in his presence.

I left school, made my way to Circular Quay by tram, thence by ferry to McMahon's Point to collect my cricket gear, and then to the Cricket Ground. A hailstorm brought that match to an unsatisfactory ending–the ground was completely covered with a thick mantle of white–but I had made my first appearance thereon under the captaincy of the famous Monty Noble, who had me fielding on the deep fine leg boundary and refrained from taking the risk of letting me have a bowl.

I felt a bit hurt when I was docked for half a day's pay when Jerry Walsh came round to deliver my cheque a week later. Even Jerry sympathized with me. He thought that I had a good case to demand my full money because I had merely acted upon instruction. Something seemed to have been whispered in my ear however that it would be more diplomatic to take the hip pocket blow without a murmur. There might reasonably be other occasions when I would be looking for a friend or two in the Leave of Absence branch down in Bridge Street.

Cricket came fairly solidly to the fore in my life after that Testimonial match. I was chosen in a New South Wales Second XI match with Victoria at the Sydney Cricket Ground. Les Gwynne led the local team which included Don Bradman, who had been brought down from the Bowral competition to take part. At our second meeting I perhaps came out on top, competitively speaking, for I was chosen to go on to the First XI for the State and Bradman was passed over. Why that happened the Lord only knows, as Bradman got going very nicely in the second innings, to show glimpses of his outstanding ability, and was out by misadventure when he hit his stumps in making a mighty pull shot. Three prospective Australian Test players made their Sydney Cricket Ground debut in that Second XI match in 1926-27. Apart from Don Bradman and me, Hans Ebeling, a future distinguished chairman of the Melbourne Cricket Club, turned out for Victoria. The three of us were later to become team-mates in Billy Woodfull's 1934 touring side.

I also played in the game which I have already mentioned, on the old Exhibition Ground in Brisbane in company with Arthur Mailey in 1927, and I played against New Zealand when Tom

Lowry's team was returning from its England tour that year.

It was Alan Kippax's first appearance as New South Wales captain when he tossed the coin with Tom Lowry. He got the job under a welter of criticism from many who thought that older men like Bardsley, Macartney, Andrews, Oldfield and Taylor should have been given preference. Kippax was a batsman of extraordinary talent who I regard as the finest example of 'classy' batsmanship of my time. His timing and placement were thrilling. It was an absolutely painless operation to have him back cut you delicately through the slips for four. I have never had a clue in all the years since it happened, why Herbie Collins did not take him to England with that worn out range of extinct volcanoes which made the tour in 1926.

My leave without pay was readily granted for these games. I had been advised of my selection in plenty of time to give the Department the required seven days' notice. But I was to get proof that the chairborne plenipotentiaries in Bridge Street had been observing my burgeoning cricket programme. A couple of days before the Christmas break-up in 1928 I was called to Head Office to be informed that my time belonged to the Education Department for teaching, not to the Australian Board of Control for cricket. They told me to be prepared for a country appointment which would land me right out of sight of cricket selectors.

Towards the end of the long vacation I was instructed by telegram to commence duties in February at Griffith, some 600 kilometres southwest of Sydney.

10 Back in the Bush

Because it was so far from the city, while I was teaching at Griffith I had an extra week's Christmas holidays. That was about the only break I ever received from the Education hierarchy, who seemed to regard talented sportsmen as mere nuisances within their regimented Department.

I was born in the west, as you know. I liked it. It was part of the contract under my bond with the Department that I would be prepared to go wherever I was directed, and I knew that every man and woman under their control was due for a three years' mandatory term of country service. I was sorry to leave behind what was shaping up to be a pleasant and successful cricket career, but I went gladly enough, resolving to spend as much time as possible mastering my wrong 'un, which I had already decided was certain to play a highly important part in my cricket career.

Looking back now, I know that I should never have felt any tingle of gladness whatever. Those three years I spent over the mountains in the service of the Education Department deprived me, I am absolutely certain, of a trip to England in 1930, and the chance to appear against Percy Chapman's 1928-29 English team in Australia.

A beautiful fourth class of about 45 boys and girls was allotted to me and I had about three months of magnificent fun with them, but it was not all plain sailing. In the first spelling test I gave them, from the prescribed list of words to be handled in third class, I got such a humiliating result that I thought fit to take the evidence to the headmaster so that he would know how the polls stood in spelling when I took over the driver's seat. He resented it. And I resented his attitude. But that didn't spoil my term with those champion kids. I still remember the fun we had in singing lessons. I taught them every Irish song I knew, and there were plenty. To hear them marching in or out of school at every recess whilst they beefed out 'The Minstrel Boy', 'The Harp that Once', 'The Last Rose of Summer' or 'Believe Me' was worth a visit to the school to hear. Even the headmaster, who had managed to give me the impression that he was singularly unimpressed with the 'O' in front of my surname, visited the class to tell my kids how he and every teacher on the staff admired their singing.

I played some local cricket in Griffith, and plenty of wickets came my way on the concrete pitches and coir mats, but by Easter time the Department decided that they needed a teacher skilled in the handling of Business Principles and Bookkeeping in the old central tablelands town of Rylstone, in the Mudgee district, and I was the one they chose.

Off I went to Rylstone, where cricket had died a natural death a few years before my arrival. The job of rejuvenating it promised to be so difficult that I was tempted to forget all about it, but on meeting a middle-aged man named George Honeysett, who had been the district's outstanding player for more than twenty years, I determined to go headlong into its re-establishment.

Together with Honeysett and another old-timer, Ken Dowd, we succeeded in building up the Rylstone team which went through the years 1928-29 and 1929-30 without suffering a defeat.

Honeysett was an extraordinary player. A left-hand batsman and right-hand off spinner, he was even at that stage quite good enough to have been chosen in any Sydney first grade side. Years before whilst visiting Mudgee and playing against the district team, Monty Noble, the great Australian all-rounder, had been so impressed that he had invited Honeysett to come to Sydney with the idea of using his talents with bat and ball to the full. George, I believe, made a reluctant effort and appeared one afternoon for Paddington,

Noble's team, but failed to reappear on the following Saturday. The city was too much for him.

The bush has lots of talented cricketers who never got the urge to get out and about. When you realize that men like Macartney, Bradman, McCabe, Walters, Bonnor, McKibbin, Turner, McCosker and Rixon were all bush boys who went the full distance in big cricket, it makes you wonder about the ones who never did cross the mountains to give themselves a run in Grade. George Honeysett was one of them. He certainly would have made good.

From Rylstone I accompanied the seventh, eighth and ninth classes to Kandos when the Department decided to turn the nearby Kandos school into an Intermediate High School. The Rylstone boys and girls travelled by bus and I took up residence at Jim McCormack's Railway Hotel near the station. There I spent a very happy year in 1930, whilst Bill Woodfull took his team of youngsters to England to regain the Ashes.

Situated a few miles south of Rylstone, Kandos was an important cement manufacturing town. It had outgrown its older neighbour, but it was taking a tremendous hiding from the Depression. I soon became aware that many of the boys and girls did not have much to eat at lunch time. It made me feel uneasy. Eating was not one of my worries, although the State Government did introduce an unemployment relief tax on all its employees to help unemployed families with children. Single people were given no help whatever. To get sustenance of the most meagre kind unmarried men and women had to go 'walkabout' from town to town. Many country towns as a result found that they could muster pretty good football and cricket teams if they kept a wary eye open for these itinerant mendicants. I know one young man, later to become a Sydney citizen of some substance, who managed to earn himself ten shillings – a dollar – nearly every week for turning out each Saturday in country sport.

The headmaster at Kandos was a sociable fellow, Bill Edgar, a returned soldier who had risen to the rank of captain in the field, and we had three wonderful women, Marjorie Brooks, Lucy Donnelly and Marg Lawson, who managed to put so much friendliness into the humdrum dispensation of knowledge that the job took on entirely new dimensions. So much so that I was genuinely unhappy about leaving for Sydney when, at the end of 1930, my three years' country service condition had been fulfilled and I was free to apply for a return appointment. Looking back now on my country term I regard myself as very lucky to have had the opportunity to get to know so many wonderful people, and to have made so many lifelong friends outback.

Roger Wotton, a parliamentarian friend of mine who is the Member for Castlereagh, invited me last year to return with him to a cricket night at Gulgong. There I met many of the men against whom I had played at Goolma in a Stag Lager Cup fixture in 1930. Goolma is one of those towns which you are likely to drive through without happening to notice anything that looks like human habitation, but it gives you the surprise such towns usually provide when you pull up to pay a courtesy call.

When I played for Kandos Wanderers we travelled by lorry the fifty odd miles, to get there ready for an early start. The Ryans and the Flannerys and the Whales lined up for Goolma and we had a memorable match. Indeed I feel that I can remember more about it even now than I do of some Test matches I played in later on. In the course of a long day Goolma won outright to retain the cup even though my bowling figures for the day's work showed 18 wickets for 90 runs. The celebration later in Ambrose Ryan's little pub alongside the Mudgee road was a memorable event, especially when we tried to give some of the local Under-21 teamsmen the smother when the police constable paid an after hour's routine duty call.

The camaraderie of the bush teams was unforgettable. The fun I had playing in places like Cudgegong, Ilford, Lue, Bylong, Mudgee, Goolma, Capertee, Rylstone and Kandos, with an occasional trip to Lithgow thrown in, has gone to make up an array of happy memories which few first-class cricketers have had the luck to amass. I can still surround myself with the faces which made the going easy and interesting for me as my cricket career marked time for three years. The Aitons and Carrolls of Griffith, the Honeysetts, the Evans and the Dowds of Rylstone, the Georges, the Watts, the Moores, the Conrys, the Riordans, the Guthries, the Newmans: just a few names passing through my mind, to all of whom I owed a soul-saving debt cricket-wise as I made my way back to Sydney so full of confidence that I welcomed the battle that lay ahead for me to return to the New South Wales team.

The Education Department might well have thought that they were sentencing me to oblivion, but my bush friends gave them the lie. Many good players in the bush had given me lots of opportunities to extend my skills. Not the least privilege given me by my teaching stretch in the bush was absolute seclusion from the slightest influence of coaching. That was of supreme importance. Not once in the backblocks did I hear one word of gratuitous advice about how to improve my bowling technique. I was given the ball and invited to get on with it – a policy, I think, that cannot possibly be improved upon.

One never hears much about country cricket these days, indeed one wonders whether the game is being played as intently as it was fifty years ago. I know that lots of those little towns which sported cricket teams long ago have ceased to perform. The disappearance was hastened when school buses came along to collect the kids to take them to a district centre for the education they needed.

Loyalty to their own little town was educated out of them. More's the pity.

At the beginning of 1931 I was appointed to teach History, English, Geography and Business Principles at Kogarah Intermediate High School.

I went back to live in North Sydney, resumed where I had left off with North Sydney First XI and bored right into the general cricket scene. I knew that I was a much more competent performer on my return. My resolve to concentrate on the wrong 'un had been so thoroughly carried into practice that I now knew that I could bowl it to line and length at will.

I regained my place in the New South Wales side in the 1930-31 season, and in 1931-32, in the glorious company of men such as Bill Woodfull, Clarrie Grimmett, Alan Kippax, Bill Ponsford, Bertie Oldfield, Jack Fingleton, Don Bradman, Bertie Ironmonger and Stan McCabe, I was picked to play for Australia in the last two Tests of the rather one-sided series against Jock Cameron's South Africans.

We won that series five Tests to nil. My contributions were satisfying, though not sensational. In the fourth Test I took 2 for 74 and 2 for 81. Clarrie Grimmett took 14 of the remaining South African wickets. In the fifth, played on a treacherous pitch in Melbourne, Australia could only manage 153 but the Springboks collapsed twice, for 45 and then for 36. I bagged 3 for 19 in their second innings. Grimmett was not called on to bowl during the match.

Don Bradman, who had made his Test debut in 1928-29, and in England in 1930 had made 974 runs in Tests at an average of 139, had five innings against the South Africans, was not out once, and scored 806 runs at an average of just over 200.

11 An Undoubted Genius

From the diminutive young man with whom I had crossed swords in 1925 at Bowral, Bradman had developed into the greatest batting sensation ever to hit the international cricket scene. His progress had been rapid and incredible. Not long after he had arrived on the Sydney scene as a member of the St George District Cricket Club he had been chosen to take his place in the New South Wales Sheffield Shield team, in which he had immediately established a commanding presence.

On holidays from my teaching job at Rylstone during the 1929 Christmas period, I made a visit to the Sydney Cricket Ground where New South Wales was playing Victoria in a Shield match. My main purpose was to take a close look at the Bowral boy.

His progress had been absolutely phenomenal. My clear memory of him as a blockbusting opponent on the Bowral concrete pitch had to be completely revised. In the bush he had relied almost entirely on his lightning-like speed in getting straight to the pitch of the ball and hitting it powerfully on either side of the wicket, but always in front of the stumps. Finesse was not then a noticeable feature of his strokemaking, but there is no real need for finesse if one is quite capable of making it to the pitch of the ball: in those conditions every delivery becomes a half-volley, which is easily despatched with a fully swung bat.

I was delighted to see that Bradman's tactics had gone through a surprising rearrangement. Although it was easy for me to recognize in him the same person who had murdered me that Saturday afternoon at Bowral a few years previously – the footwork was still an outstanding feature of his batting set up – what impressed me most was that he had thoroughly learned the art of moving onto the back foot. This gave him twofold advantages: he could defend against the good length ball much more reliably, and the range of his scoring shots had been widened to include the run-scoring opportunities behind the wicket.

As I took my seat on the Hill it almost seemed to me that he had noted my arrival, because to impress me and demand my very close attention he went back on his toes to get Victorian pace bowler Hans Ebeling away to the fine leg boundary just as though he had been doing the same thing all his life. It was the first time I had seen him play that shot. I saw it hundreds of times in the years which lay ahead.

His almost immediate reaction to turf wickets and to consistently accurate bowling had been his recognition of the need to get safely and defiantly on to the back foot as his major batting ploy. All those who never had the animated experience of bowling at him have, so it seems, been most impressed with his speed and cleverness in leaving the crease and moving well down the pitch in search of his prey. To those people I hasten to give the assurance that the forward move was not the secret of the maestro's success. Hidden securely in his mental clockwork was an extraordinary facility for summing up the length and speed of a delivery simultaneously, so it seemed, with the ball's release from the bowler's hand. This gave him the immeasurable advantage of deciding immediately whether to move on to the front or the back foot. You can take it from me, who bowled at every batsman on the international first-class scene between 1931 and 1938, that the toughest batting proposition facing any bowler is the discerning batsman who know just when to use back-foot play.

One of my first jobs in facing up to an unknown batsman was to find out without delay how secure he was when forced onto the back foot in defending his wicket. If he showed me the slightest sign that his technique in that regard was faulty I couldn't get the ball back again quickly enough to concentrate on the dissection of the case. Give me a batsman, I used to think, who could not defend stoutly on the back foot, and I would have been prepared to give a written guarantee that I would get him out at least once every over I bowled at him. You can therefore imagine my surprise and unbounded admiration for the young Bradman when I observed him going on to his back foot so confidently, not only to defend, but also to take many runs on the leg side with a newly found leg glance and a powerful hook fine of square leg. On the off side he had learned to get right back to give himself the opportunity to use the late cut, another new shot in his repertoire. As he batted that day I realized that the bush boy had already become a world-beater.

As a batsman, he was an undoubted genius. Bowling at him was a grand experience for a thoughtful bowler. He seemed to have a ready and highly reliable answer for everything a bowler tried. Should a bowler 'put one over' him it was best that it capture his wicket, for the same bowler could bet that the same trick would not work again during the day.

For example, bowling to him one day on the Sydney Cricket Ground, I decided to try him out with an uncharacteristic change of pace. Holding the ball so loosely in my right hand that I began to doubt my chances of keeping hold of it whilst I made my grooved approach to the crease, I went through the motions which would be telling him that I intended to deliver my accustomed leg break. The ball landed on a length in line with the middle and leg stumps and Bradman, showing all the signs of having been surprised, scuffled with unusual diffidence to the ball and smothered it safely enough in forward defence. His wide-eyed, hurried look in my direction conveyed the dismal tidings that he was well aware that I had tried to do the dirty on him and that he would be on the lookout for that particular ball for the remainder of the day's operations.

In 1930 Bradman flattened England's cricket ego. He got runs whenever they were needed and in such copious supply that he came to be recognized as the most formidable foe English bowling had ever faced. Poor Maurice Tate, whom I regard with Alec

Bedser as the greatest fast-medium bowler I have seen, was completely nonplussed. At the end of a career which had seen him rise to the very top of the bowling ladder, Tate finally admitted that he had no answer for the young Australian's outstanding batting gift.

Bradman left English cricket lying in shambles in 1930 and returned home to the plaudits of his countrymen, who treated him as though he was a gift from the gods. Devoted well-wishers gave him not a moment's peace. Recognition in crowded city streets precipitated embarrassing exhibitions of public adulation. Bradman must often have longed for the peace and quiet he knew existed in his peaceful mountain home town of Bowral. Those days were over for him forever. He simply had to accustom himself to the nauseating glare of publicity which is part and parcel of a hero's life style. He was not an extroverted sort of person in private life. It was virtually impossible for him to appear in public. His presence in a public bar would have been a sensation. I can't really imagine what would have happened. He was denied many of the normal pleasures of daily life. Those of us who were close enough to him to recognize the signs knew that it was hell for him.

For myself I was short-tempered enough to resent the few intrusions upon my own privacy when unknown well-wishers recognized me, and roared out congratulations or commiserations or advice across a crowded bar. It generally meant that I took quick delivery of my beer and made off in search of another place where I might relax in peace. Bradman couldn't do that.

I remember an experience in South Africa in 1935-36, where I came face to face with a situation which Bradman faced every time he poked his nose outside the door.

After arriving at the Carlton Hotel in Johannesburg, I set out to take the lift to the street, having settled safely into my allotted quarters on the top floor. Pressing the lift button I held the door open in the manner prescribed for a youngish redheaded woman whose face was becomingly covered with freckles. Having acknowledged each other's existence with the exchange of a few appropriate pleasantries, I stood aside to allow her to enter the hotel's main lounge. To my dismay the place was jam-packed with people. Their expectant faces told me that they were there to give the once over either to the young redhead, or to me. Suspecting the former, and fortified by the knowledge that all the locals knew that we had come to town without Don Bradman, I walked embarrassedly through the throng. I was relieved to find that all eyes followed the redhead–any that landed on me seemed to be merely inquisitive. The explanation was forthcoming before we reached the desk to hand in our keys. A girl in the crowd within my hearing asked, 'And who's the skinny bloke with her?'

'It must be Mr Gracie Fields,' someone replied.

I had the opporunity of relating my personal reaction to Gracie when I met her at breakfast the next morning. She laughed her high-pitched laugh when I told her that I had momentarily suspected the crowd thought I was Don Bradman. She told me that she was used to such crowd behaviour and that it helped her career along and was very good for her ego.

I wonder whether it would have made a difference to Bradman's career if he had been able to lap up the unquenchable eagerness with which cricket crowds tried desperately hard just to touch him.

12 Bodyline

Though I am the only Australian still living who played in each of the five bodyline Tests in 1932-33, I feel that I should apologize for writing about that hackneyed subject at length. Like many other people I feel that too much has been written by too many people, most of whom, faced with the difficulties in researching the subject, have been prone to let their imaginations and patriotic feelings run wild. In other words, I might as well say straight away that lots of utter rubbish has been written on this perplexing subject. But in fairness to three mates of mine who faced the barrier in those five perilous Tests, Bill Woodfull our gallant captain, Victor Richardson, and Stan McCabe, I think this is one occasion on which it behoves me to jot down the sequence of events of that nerve-shattering season.

To set the scene in its proper perspective one must try to look at it through an English cricketer's eyes. Here was a young Australian, gifted beyond belief in both batting ability and physical durability, who looked likely to go on with his joyful task of crucifying England's best bowlers for twenty years. Centuries meant so little to him that he carried on to double centuries and treble centuries if need be. The future looked bleak for English cricket.

The time was ripe for a bit of hard, positive thinking. Englishmen have never been slow to rise to the bait of a thoroughly provocative situation.

In a famous quarrel they had with an overbearingly powerful monarch three hundred years before, they had come to light with a champion named Oliver Cromwell. Charles I had found out in 1649 that his fellow Englishmen were hard nuts to crack when they really got their backs up. He paid for it on the chopping block. And when the brilliant young Frenchman Napoleon Bonaparte controlled all the scoring shots available throughout Europe in a time which saw England face to face with extinction, they came up once again with Horatio Nelson, the pocket-sized sailor who won the final test at Trafalgar, leaving the stage clear for Wellington and Blucher to do the mopping up work on the sticky wicket that was Europe in the early nineteenth century.

None but a fool would underrate England's resourcefulness. Too often throughout their history they have shown that it is easy for them – comes naturally perhaps – to conjure up the scheme required to bring relief.

Here then they were hard pressed. This modern Napoleon hailing from the South Seas had freebooted it throughout their beautiful countryside laying waste their cricket grounds as he waged his brilliant 1930 batting campaign. This had to be met with true British fighting spirit. They came to light once again by pinning their faith on a gaunt, hard-faced six-footer named Douglas Jardine – born in India, educated at Winchester and Oxford, and already known as an unrelenting competitor steeped in the art of waging an all-out battle in which no holds were barred.

Rockley Wilson, his cricket master at the highbrowed school of Winchester, had little cause to like Australia, he had an unhappy time on tour here as a member of John Douglas's 1920-21 team. Wilson sounded an ominous warning when he heard that Jardine had been chosen to lead England for the 1932-33 tour.

'Douglas Jardine will regain the Ashes but England stands a good chance of losing a colony,' was his reaction to the news.

No one in Australia took any notice at the time, of course, but how interesting it is now to look back and try to piece together the thoughts contained in those few words. Whether anybody ever interviewed Wilson to find out what he had to say about it all after the tumult and the shouting of the 1932-33 season had died down,

I regret to admit that I have never been able to discover. He was certainly entitled to say, 'I told you so.'

Similiarly, when England named its players for the invasion of the Great South Land in 1932, nobody was the least bit worried about the composition of the side. Their batting as usual looked good. Herbert Sutcliffe, Walter Hammond, Duleepsinhji, Bob Wyatt, Maurice Leyland, the Nawab of Pataudi, Jardine, Eddie Paynter and Les Ames made up a formidable batting wall that would be hard for Australian bowlers to scale. Their bowling consisted of three quickies: Harold Larwood, Bill Voce – of whom both Stan McCabe and Victor Richardson spoke highly after having faced his fast left-arm inswingers at Trent Bridge in 1930 – and Gubby Allen, the surprisingly quick right-hander who had already made his Test debut against Australia.

Nobody raised even a querulous eyebrow at the team's personnel. We self-satisfied Australians remained secure in the comforting thought that we had the 'little fellow', as we called him, on our side.

The first misadventure was that the unlucky Duleepsinhji, nephew of the great Ranjitsinhji, was found to be suffering from a spot on the lung and withdrew from the team to seek a cure in the Swiss Alps. That was a dreadful blow for England. Every man who had played against the gifted Indian Prince in the 1930 series in England had spoken of him in the highest possible terms. He was, they said, a brilliant attacking batsman whose game seemed specially designed for success on Australian pitches.

We were inclined to commiserate with England over the loss of Duleep, however we were surprised when England's selectors announced his replacement. To replace a world-class batsman, they chose lanky Bill Bowes, the bespectacled Yorkshire bouncer bowler who had so recently raised the ire of Jack Hobbs, England's legendary batting hero, when he let go a barrage at the veteran's head in the course of a County match at the Oval. This selection needed a bit of thought. What were the English up to?

I have read and listened to lots of theories about what had gone on in England, where tactics for the tour had been quite obviously altered in the space of a few days. At the Sydney Cricket Ground, on the afternoon when that news was received, I heard Bradman offer the opinion that he thought that the Tests looked like being turned into shooting galleries when the Englishmen took the field. Every first-class player in Australia realized that the English were up to fun and games of some sort and every single one of us knew that whatever it was it was absolutely certain to involve Bradman.

Yes, I had heard about the final Test at the Oval in 1930 when Bradman was supposed to have flinched against Larwood, who had made the ball lift dangerously on a wet wicket, but I was completely unmoved by that. My limited experience of wet wickets had shown me that no batsman was really worth a damn when the ball was rising at varying heights. A wet wicket in Melbourne on which 'Dainty' Ironmonger had taken five South African wickets for seven runs the previous season had taught me that no real bowler should regard it as too much of a hardship if eleven Bradmans were lined up against him on such a wicket.

A wet Australian wicket is a surpassingly horrifying experience for batsmen. The ball will rise chin-high from a delivery pitched right up near the blockhole. It is futile to use the feet. The one method to use is to hit like blazes straight into the pitch of the ball and hope that catches take a longer time than usual to go to hand. Scientific batting is absolutely of no avail. I once saw Walter Hammond perform bravely on a Melbourne sticky, when he tried in vain to cope with accurate medium-paced bowling. He was disguised so completely in protective gear worn under his clothing that he resembled the character in the ads for Michelin tyres, but he still finished his gallant innings bruised from head to foot. If a ball bounced dangerously high, and almost every delivery did that, Hammond took his bat out of its way and allowed the ball to hit him on the body.

But surely the Englishmen were not banking on a wet Australian summer. We knew that their hopes were forlorn enough to be pinned onto the remotest eventuality, but to rely on a wet summer in this country was going a bit too far.

Australian wickets at that time were rock hard. The ball made not the slightest indentation, even on the first day when some of the moisture used in preparation would be likely still to exist.

One must bear in mind that pitches those days were not covered.

Some tarpaulin was used. At the end of a day's play the ground staff would lay fourteen-feet pieces at either end of the pitch, sufficient to protect the batsman's stance position at the crease and extending far enough behind it to give the bowler about ten feet of firm ground for the last few strides of his run up. In preparation, the groundsman was allowed to cover his pitch at will with the idea of producing the finest and toughest surface within his power. But as soon as the captains tossed the laws of the international contests laid down that all protective covering should be removed and from thence onward until the match was decided there should be no covering used. So the groundsmen had to prepare their wickets knowing that they were going to have to last for a long time.

That makes it easier to understand why the English tour administration of 1932 pinned all their faith on the rock-like nature of the pitches in our country. They were absolutely right on the ball. It was a simple matter to get the ball up high. All their fast bowlers had to do was to bowl it short and make it bounce.

But physically it was not an easy job for bowlers who had performed mainly on soft English turf. In Australia it was customary for bowlers to suffer bruised heels, lost toenails, and swollen knees, and to regard such as no more than the fortunes of war. To amplify this a little from personal experience, I lost the left big toenail seventeen years in succession. Just as it had regenerated becomingly, as I thought, by about September, I would set about its annihilation all over again.

To make certain then that they did not run out of fast bowling manpower the English selectors decided to bring four pacemen.

The English, we knew in our hearts, were not banking on rain-affected wickets. Theirs was another ploy, a departure that was to set the game alight. If the wickets were not going to help the ball to bounce high enough to worry the Australian champion batsman, they would encourage their bowlers to get the ball to bounce head-high by the only method available to them: by pitching it short, in line with the leg stump.

The point I wish to make at this stage is that the policy of bowling short and corroding batting confidence by hostile field placing was set down hard and fast before the English side arrived in Western Australia in October 1932. Arthur Carr of Notts had already brought his name into prominence with his canny handling of his team-mates Harold Larwood and Bill Voce. Larwood and Voce had lunched with Carr and Douglas Jardine at the Piccadilly Hotel long before they had set out for Australia. I'll bet that the price of coal at the mineheads was not the topic up for discussion at that festive board. Jardine, I am certain, went through all his campaign plans meticulously before he left home. It was he, I feel sure, who suggested that Bill Bowes, who couldn't bat for nuts, should replace Duleepsinhji, who was the second best batsman, after Hammond, in the original side.

The original selection, which included Duleep, gave us no hint that a bouncer campaign was contemplated. The final arrangement with Bowes coming into the team positively reeked of it. The late selection of Bowes suggests the intrigue which went on during the few weeks immediately before the team was due to sail. Had one been able to keep one's eyes carefully trained on Jardine in those few weeks I reckon that he would have been found to have been conferring with every person he thought could offer help about bowling fast and short, and better still, who had gained some experience on Australian wickets.

I am sure it is safe to say that to Jardine, possibly with occasional help from Herbert Sutcliffe who left no doubt in our minds that he was an enthusiastic fellow traveller, goes the credit, or discredit, for the placing of the field which supported the bouncer bowling. Without that field the bouncer campaign would have failed hopelessly, let there be no doubt whatever about that.

The tour began, as usual, with a match against Western Australia in which Jardine picked a near Test eleven. This is the usual ploy at the commencement of a long tour. It is best to let all the key players blow the cobwebs away after several lotus-eating weeks on board ship.

Larwood was given a run of course. He bowled six overs, and took a couple of wickets. This game was followed by a match against a Combined Australian XI, made up mainly of players from

Western Australia, with a few stars from the other States. In this type of fixture it is usual for both sides to play politics: for instance both Bradman and McCabe, Australia's two outstanding batsmen, were chosen to take a good look at the English attack, and Jack Fingleton, an up-and-coming Australian opener with one Test against South Africa under his belt, was sent along with them on the train journey across Australia to sharpen his talents for the coming season. But politics demanded that no established Australian Test bowler would make the journey. The Englishmen were not invited to sample our wares. I for one, who had just entered the cricket limelight, was left at home, as was Clarence Grimmett. Neither Larwood nor Voce played for the MCC in the Combined XI game.

Gubby Allen and Walter Hammond took the new ball, supported by spinners Tommy Mitchell and Hedley Verity. England got a huge score to which Jardine contributed 98 before he was caught by McCabe off Bradman's lofted leg break bowling, an incident which must have nettled his lordship cruelly. (I am sure that Bradman, at the end of his incredible career, must have been disappointed to have been deprived of the privilege of dealing with his own bowling. He would have done enormous damage to it in a couple of overs.)

Jardine, however, would have been delighted when a rain-damaged pitch allowed Verity to collect seven wickets, including Bradman's for 3, to make the Combined XI follow on in a drawn game. Jardine would have left Perth perfectly happy. His batsmen had all had good pratice there, and his bowlers had plenty of opportunities to get themselves fit. He may have regretted the fact that young Fingleton had grabbed the chance to build up confidence with scores of 29 and 53 not out, but Bradman's twice out for 13 runs would have more than made up for it. To have got the boy wonder twice cheaply in the one game without having to use his strike bowlers must have come as a most pleasant surprise.

Against South Australia, England collected over 600 runs with the skipper himself this time contributing 108. Grimmett collected 4 wickets in 40 overs. The Englishmen scored a lot of runs from his bowling, but they batted first on a pitch traditionally hostile to slow bowling on the first two days of a match. South Australia were beaten by an innings despite captain Victor Richardson's first innings' century. Larwood was given only 5 overs and Bowes, in his first tour appearance, was given 32 overs. So far Bill Voce had been kept safely on ice.

Then on to Victoria and the east, where once again Douglas resorted to politics. Larwood and Bowes were spelled but Bill Voce, appearing for the first time, was given 25 overs. England won this too, by an innings, with 203 against the name of their star batsman, Walter Hammond.

Now came one of the crucial fixtures of the tour. Jardine chose the game against an Australian XI including Bradman, played towards the end of November at the Melbourne Cricket Ground where the pitch at that time gave plenty of help to fast bowlers, to test his new bowling theory. The fast bowlers Larwood, Voce, Allen and Bowes were all picked, but, ever the politician, Jardine chose not to take part in the match himself.

He didn't even watch the game. He visited friends in the country for a spot of fishing. His deputy, the quiet, reserved, reliable Bob Wyatt had the privilege of unveiling Douglas Jardine's contribution to cricket folklore. One wonders why the English captain chose to be absent. Perhaps in case the plan backfired: if Bradman had ripped off a brilliant century Bob Wyatt could have carried the can. Or perhaps it was to give the Australian team a chance to ponder the likely developments to the new policy when the captain himself returned to the driver's seat.

The match was drawn, but the result is of little significance. The important thing for England was that Bradman's wicket fell twice to Larwood's bowling for 49 runs. And much more important even than that was the fact that the great Australian batsman had shown unmistakeable signs of having been rattled during his introduction to the hostile bowling of the great fast bowler, with its accompanying ring of close-in supporting fieldsmen.

Leo O'Brien, Victoria's determined left-handed opening batsman, top scored with 46 runs and in so doing laid his claim for selection in Tests, and in fact the England XI collapsed for only 60 in their second innings in the face of some inspired swing bowling from Lisle Nagel, who took 8 wickets for only 32. But the match fulfilled Jardine's prospects of campaign success handsomely. His plan had succeeded beyond the hopes he had any right to expect. His three fast bowlers had performed creditably and Bradman, he would have been thinking, showed signs of becoming amenable to English discipline.

The scene then changed to Sydney, where I met them for the first time, to find some English players were openly skiting that they had Bradman well and truly on the run when Larwood bowled him in the Melbourne second innings. Larwood did not play against New South Wales, but Bradman, by then in the middle of a raging row with the Australian Board over his writing commitments, was again a failure by his own standards, making only 18 and 23. By the time the New South Wales match was won by them by an innings, the Englishmen had every right to think that events had gone along absolutely to order since the tour began. By then Bradman had been to the wicket six times against them and they had managed to dispose of him for the incredible tally of 103 runs. Normally he would have been expected to have scored 103 in the first session of the first day that he appeared against them.

They would have been wide awake to the threatening form of Fingleton, who apart from that fine opening innings in Perth had batted right through the New South Wales first innings for 119, and had withstood the aggressive bouncer tactics of Bill Voce and the wiles of Maurice Tate. They might too have noticed that a bowler named O'Reilly had made a threatening debut by collecting 4 wickets for 86 runs off 46 overs against them in Sydney. But these two events understandably were nothing compared with their Bradman result. I had the feeling after the New South Wales match that the whole English team had begun to feel that they had the game sewn up—that they were home and hosed. And to make matters worse, in the few days between the New South Wales game and the first Test, both played in Sydney, rumours began to fly thick and fast about Bradman and his future involvement in the season's proceedings. Where some of them came from heaven only knows. True, he wasn't well, but I remember hearing that pernicious anaemia had been diagnosed and that he would never again appear on a cricket field.

In any case, he was unavailable for the first Test, which England won by ten wickets. That match was made immortal by Stan McCabe, who against Larwood and Voce bowling bodyline to a packed leg-side field, almost destroyed Jardine's new theory. McCabe scored 187 not out in our first innings and so demoralized the English bouncer attack that Jardine must have had irritating doubts about the ultimate success of his campaign. It was an inspiring sight to me as I watched that 22-year-old boy, my close friend, getting down the pitch after both Larwood and Voce, even though they persisted in pitching short and bouncing them at him. He so dominated the English pace attack that he forced Jardine to remove his men from the close catching positions.

As many as eight fieldsmen were sometimes positioned on the leg side of the field for bodyline, whereas these days no bowler, even a slow bowler, is allowed more than five on that side under the present law, which was later adopted with the purpose of outlawing the bodyline theory. Six men were set in the close positions, silly mid-on, silly leg, short square leg, and then three leg slips in a circle reaching around to the 'keeper, Les Ames, who lined up with them to make a cordon seven men strong. The close men in front of the bat stood ready to snap up the propped shot off the middle of a defensive bat trying to cope with a head-high 'sconner'. The only way to deal safely with such a delivery was to forget the bat and duck from the knees for dear life. The other fieldsmen were there to deal with the edges a powerfully swung bat might find during an adventurous innings.

As well as the six men in close on the leg side, there were two in the deep, at deep square leg and deep fine leg, in case the adventurous batsman, quick on his feet and capable of moving inside the line of the ball and hooking powerfully, chose to go on the attack. These men were placed for the catch which must almost inevitably eventuate if the batsman tries to hook consistently short pitched bowling.

So the bodyline field devised by Douglas Jardine made the use of the bat a hopeless proposition for even the most gifted, fleet-footed batsman. Consistently attaining shoulder-height or higher, and bowled accurately just a trifle outside the leg stump so that it threatened life and limb, and launched at the bowler's top speed, most Australian batsmen found it quite useless to present their bat either in defence of their stumps, or in self-preservation, or in attack, when the 'sconner' was bowled.

Because of the consequent ducking from harm's way, it is no wonder that bodyline bowlers hit the stumps so often. It is a relatively simple matter to get a quick yorker straight through to the stumps of a batsman already grooved intently upon ducking. The argument used by English critics of Australian batting performances, that their great bowler Larwood hit the stumps 14 times, cuts no ice with me if it is used to try to justify the argument that the great English bowler did not drop the ball short so consistently as bodyline detractors have stated. Those 14 clean bowled victims out of his 33 Test wickets in the series should not be taken out of their context: he clean bowled me four times, and twice he hit the stumps of my Rabbitoh mate Bert Ironmonger, who was a worse bat even than I was. We made a substantial contribution to his total of 14. Bradman alone fell victim more than once to Larwood's surprise packet, a fast good length ball straight on line.

Larwood collected the wickets of all but two Australians who were chosen to play in Tests that eventful season. Tim Wall, our fast bowler, refused to dip his batting colours to his speed rival. Tim indeed played a magnificent batting hand in Sydney, holding up his number eleven wicket whilst Stan McCabe added substantially to his score. The other Australian who never departed the scene at Larwood's direction was Len Darling, who played in the fourth and fifth Tests. That quick-talking, square-chinned, pugnacious left-hander, who reckoned his sister could have dealt successfully with Larwood's brand of bowling, never once in my presence admitted that speed bowling was of more consequence than cold chicken. With him it was not idle talk. His famous hook shot took lots of paint off boundary fences in Australia, England and South Africa. I still have a wonderful recollection of the memorable assault he made on England's new found bowling star Ken Farnes, whom he took apart at Chelmsford in the County match with Essex early in the 1934 tour of England.

But it was Stan McCabe who belted the heart out of 'scone theory' that afternoon in Sydney, when he turned on one of the most inspiring performances seen on a cricket field. McCabe was a retiring person, never one to push his own barrow. He was just a rosy-faced, twinkle-eyed, sparse-thatched boy when he ripped bodyline apart. He held no theory about it whatever. He just sailed in defying everything that the bouncer bowlers could do, and the next morning he went on with it.

I became even more closely observant as my time to face the batting music drew near, but apart from a pious faith in the helpful intervention of Dame Fortune I held out little hope for success with the bat. McCabe kept the record crowd in a constant state of uproar. To get a better view, the crowd sitting on the asphalt in front of the Sheridan and Brewongle Stands pulled most of the palings off the boundary fence. The only people not cheering madly were those hanging on tenaciously with both hands to the steel fences around the Ladies' Stand, next to our players' room. Stan's mother was seated high up in the stand, ably squired by McCabe senior, all the way down from Grenfell, and under careful instructions to keep mother under constraint should Stan happen to impede the progress of a sconner with his helmetless head.

Victor Richardson battled bravely and well for 49, then whilst McCabe was sailing past his century Clarrie Grimmet bravely held up one end and occasionally enjoyed himself by trying out his famous back cut from afar. Voce had Grimmett caught behind, then Larwood bowled Lisle Nagel first ball. I can still see the off stump cartwheeling away as the Victorian giant – he was over six feet six – was half-way through his shot.

McCabe was 127 not out when my turn came to walk weak-kneed towards the centre of the Sydney Cricket Ground carrying a bat with me. As I made my diffident way from the dressing-room door, my captain, Woodfull, God bless him, said, 'Listen carefully, Tiger. I want you, above all, not to get hit.'

What a relief! Could any shivering batsman ever have been

presented with a more reassuring exit than that? I have always been quick to offer him my undying gratitude for those few kind words in my biggest moment of crisis. As I walked out into the brilliant sunlight I was surprised to see McCabe leave the wicket and come walking out in my direction. It passed quickly through my mind that he was coming out to say a word or two like, 'Surely to God it's not as bad as all that, skipper. Have you got to send this bloke in so early in the day? What chance have we got?' in remonstration to Woodfull himself. Then I remembered that he was my very best cricket friend and that he probably had a few compassionate words to say to me in distress. He did. 'Good luck, Tige, get right in behind him,' he said. 'He won't waste a sconner on you. Good luck, mate.' That was all.

I knew that he was dead right. Had I been in Larwood's place I would not have dreamed of wasting energy on a bouncer to a big awkward flat-footed number ten batsman playing in his first Test against England. His words however were inspiring. Realizing that he could do with some support in rubbing English noses into our Bulli soil, I strode manfully to the Randwick end where I took block from umpire George Borwick, dug myself in and looked around the field with that discerning eye which I had noticed was the hallmark of proficiency with the bat.

Larwood, it seemed to me, was waiting far away in the Paddington distance with the expectant air that a bowler adopts when he senses a first-class opportunity of finishing the day with a hat-trick.

He came steaming in and I moved right across behind my bat, held perfectly straight in defence of my centre stump. Just before he delivered the ball something hit the middle of my bat with such force that it was almost dashed from my hands. It was the ball. With such sleight-of-hand tricks going on I realized that I had taken up a position entirely irreconcilable with my promise to my captain. It was there and then that I realized how fundamental it is for a young player to carry out his leader's instructions absolutely to the letter. I firmly resolved never to offend again. I looked down the pitch to find McCabe staring at me with that provocative twinkle in his eye. I just shook my head. He nodded back. He understood. I hadn't seen a thing.

That was the only time in that series that I really got right behind my bat in an attempt to deal with Larwood. He collected my wicket five times during the series. You can guess how loudly the great English bowler would have complained to our selectors had they dared to drop me from the side.

That Sydney Test taught me that English batsmen had decided to put the lid on my bowling and to take not the slightest chance against me, as my tactics were quite new to them. They were, so Leyland told me later, mystified that I could at such pace get my leg break to turn on a hard Australian pitch, and that I could also turn and hide the action of my wrong 'un. Consequently they had decided to force me to earn my wickets the hard way by taking as few risks as possible.

Early in England's innings I got the inside edge of Sutcliffe's bat with a wrong 'un which deflected straight to the base of the middle and off stumps. The bails didn't come off. Oldfield couldn't believe his eyes. Neither could Richardson nor McCabe, both fielding close in.

Sutcliffe was the toughest competitor I ever faced in a Test match. He was not unusually gifted, except in his unrelenting purpose to grind a bowler into the grass. Never did he pick my wrong 'un. Should the ball happen to duck away from his finely placed defence and wend its way through my slips field he would smilingly take the single and look slightingly down his nose at me as he did so. If I delivered a ball outside the line of the off stump, no matter how narrow the margin, he dobbed his left pad down the wicket in front of it and kept his bat aloft over his left shoulder.

I loved bowling at him. It was an exquisite feeling to get one past his defensive bat. His humiliation made the day for me. Whenever he got close to misjudging the position of his off stump in using his left pad to my wrong 'un I made it a practice to appeal raucously for a leg-before decision. To my great joy, this nettled him immensely.

In our very first Test encounter – he went on to make 194 in that Sydney Test – he muttered to me that I must conduct my bowling job much more responsibly if I were to make a name for myself in the game. I got the message that he was really objecting to my loud appeals. Later as I was leaving the field with 'Yorker' Richardson, Herbert came over and said, 'Take no notice of me, Bill. Sometimes I feel that I need a good kick in the stern for the things I say out there in the middle.'

'My bloody oath, Herbie, I often feel like giving you one myself,' said Yorker.

We were soundly defeated in that first Test of the series, but neither side had shown any real advantage. Larwood, in collecting 10 wickets, had begun menacingly. So had McCabe. Bill Voce took 6 wickets but had shown that he could be hit. Over five runs per over were scored against him when McCabe was at the wicket, and throughout the whole innings almost four runs per over were averaged against him. Luck had gone heavily with England when Sutcliffe's bails refused to drop, which allowed him to add 150 more runs to his score. Apart from McCabe, Fingleton and Richardson were the only Australians to bat with any real confidence.

Three weeks later, after the Englishmen had spent their Christmas holidays with two Tasmanian fixtures, we lined up again in Melbourne for the second Test. The Australian selectors had already begun to lose their nerve. Delighted with the comforting thought that Bradman's health had been completely restored in the interval, they decided that Bill Ponsford, a batsman of the highest possible calibre, could do the twelfth man's job and that Alan Kippax and Lisle Nagel should disappear from the scene altogether. Leo O'Brien came into the side with Bradman, and old Bert 'Dainty' Ironmonger, then 51 years of age, was chosen to invigorate the attack. To emphasize the selectors' state of bewilderment, Woodfull's appointment as captain was not made official until a few minutes before the time came to toss the coin.

That was my best Test from the point of view of personal satisfaction. I came out of it with 10 wickets, and Australia won by 111 runs.

It began badly. Opening with Fingleton, Woodfull had scored 10 with the total at 29 when Allen bowled him. Thirty odd runs later O'Brien was unfortunately run out. It was the first time he had batted in partnership with Fingleton, who had a disconcerting habit of taking a few steps forward after contacting the ball, as though he were starting for the run. Batting with him – unaware of this peculiarity – a tense batsman backing up could easily land himself in trouble, and that's just what happened to O'Brien that morning.

The big crowd barracked Fingleton unmercifully as a result, and were in such a boisterous state that they hardly seemed aware that Bradman had come to the crease. But then came the most animated scene of the whole dramatic season. Bill Bowes was in charge of the Richmond end, bowling his fairly ordinary fast-medium stuff. He had not yet developed into the fine bowler he was when, with Ken Farnes, he carried the English fast attack against Australia in England in 1938. Realizing that Bradman had arrived in his rightful place in the middle of their well-loved MCG, the Melbourne crowd finally gave him a tumultuous welcome, hoping I suppose that he would carry on from where McCabe had left off in Sydney.

The crowd in those days had to put up with spartan conditions. The big South Stand had not yet been built, and most of the 68,000 stood throughout the day on the outer which was covered with asphalt approaching melting point.

Everybody expected the Australian hero to make a triumphal return after his first Test indisposition. And there was big Bill Bowes realizing no doubt that here he was being presented with the opportunity to justify the reasoning that accounted for his invitation to tour. Bowes' first ball, pitched short and directed approximately in line with the middle and off stumps, was one which Bradman would have been expected to deal with nonchalantly, but completely out of character the champion made a quick shuffling movement in the general direction of point, playing the semblance of a hook shot as he went. He made contact all right, but the ball sped from the inside edge straight into the stumps. He was out first ball.

I have read an English account of this incident which took hundreds of words to describe the surpassing skill of Bowes in bringing about Bradman's downfall. On the other hand Australians think that their champion merely 'pulled the wrong rein', causing himself to badly mishandle a long hop. Strangely, this was Bowes' only Test in the series, and Bradman's was his only wicket. Still, this one ball certainly justified Bowes' place on the tour.

Bradman went on to get a splendid second innings century which played a crucial part in Australia's winning the Test to square the series one all. That century–103 from a total of 191–was Bradman's most important contribution to the series. The Melbourne pitch gave no inspiration whatever to the four English pace bowlers who found it almost impossible to make the ball rise dangerously, and the Australian spinners finally won the game, dismissing England for 169 and 139.

So much has been written, said and screened about the third Test: all that remains for me to do is to give my own participant's account of it. The series stood at one all when we lined up in Adelaide, where the crowd is usually as staid as the Oval is scenic. No one expected fireworks. The local pitch had long been regarded as the most docile on the Australian scene. It was an impossibility, we all thought, for the English fast bowlers to extract much fun from it. We Australian spinners knew that we could play an influential part only if we could get the Englishmen on a wearing pitch towards the end of the match, when it was quite likely that a spinning ball would bite. For my part my hopes were centred on our skipper's chances of winning the toss, and my side batting first.

The Adelaide crowd, who turned up in record numbers, were all agog for the combat before the game started. Indeed they turned up in force at one of the English practice sessions and set about giving Jardine larry-dooley as they looked on behind the nets arranged in the area below the scoreboard. So poorly did the English captain regard this display that he arranged for the crowd to be absent when his next practice session took place. This early display of temper from outside the boundary fences showed quite clearly that South Australian enthusiasts were well aware of the general trend of the bitter campaign that was being waged, and it clearly indicated that there would be lots of trouble brewing if Australian players became targets in the bouncer parade.

Jardine won the toss, and as things turned out that was a lucky break for our batsmen. England batted first, and as luck would have it Adelaide's pitch misbehaved badly in the first session of play. Once again Woodfull threw me the new ball to partner Wall in the swing attack. From the very first delivery the ball was lifting dangerously from a good length. We soon realized that groundsman Alby Wright had been extraordinarily lavish in his use of the watering can. Within a couple of overs we Australians, especially our batsmen, were counting our blessings over the luck of the toss. Had England's tearaway pacemen operated on that flighty strip the Lord alone knows what our casualties could have been. Four English wickets fell for 36 runs in the first session. Tim Wall got two of them and Ironmonger and I one each.

Jardine had opened the batting himself with Sutcliffe. Wall clean bowled the captain, and for good measure he caught Sutcliffe off my bowling for us to have two wickets down for 16 runs. He lifted our hopes even higher when he got a ball on his accustomed length, aimed at Walter Hammond's leg stump, to lift with such surprising hostility that the English champion dollied it straight above his head for Oldfield to grab it gratefully. I knew instinctively that Hammond was embarrassed and badly rattled, but I was not prepared for the comment he made as he passed disconsolately on his way to the pavilion. 'If that's what the bloody game's coming to, I've had enough of it,' was his solemn finding.

All the liveliness disappeared from the pitch during the lunch hour, and England's score grew apace to 7 for 236 per favour of Ames, Wyatt and Leyland, by the close of the first day's play. They were all out for 341 the next day – a day which made its way into cricket history.

Australia started little better than England. Jack Fingleton collected a duck which was the first of his dreaded 'pair' for the match. Soon after that, an awful hullabaloo arose from the Adelaide crowd when Woodfull was floored by a Larwood delivery which hit him high on the chest. Already frantic with indignation, the crowd went berserk when Jardine signalled his lethal leg-side fielding brigade to fill their vital postings as Woodfull prepared to face up again after the fearful blow. That dreadful display of heartlessness was more than anyone could take without some show of discontent. Sitting in the safety of the Australian dressing room I quickly summed it up then as the lousiest thing I had ever seen in my cricket career. I still class it as such.

The game went on through its six days' course and England came out well on top with a 338 run surplus. But the victory was not all theirs. Indeed I feel quite sure that England will have long since come to the conclusion that the match was one Test victory that they would dearly like to have expunged from the record. So far as the Australian players were concerned, Woodfull's famous message to Plum Warner, who came to offer sympathy as Woodfull lay on a table receiving treatment for his injuries, said everything which needed to be said. The words were eloquently expressed, in gentlemanly style, by as brave a man as ever walked onto a cricket field.

Then the cablegrams began to pulsate backwards and forwards and such a magnificent donnybrook arose that we poor insignificant Australian players who had been copping everything bar the bucket so far, joyously realized that there was punishment enough for everybody to share: Jardine especially, Larwood, Plum Warner, the Press and–God forbid!–the MCC.

Everyone in our dressing room knew all about that first Australian cable that contained the dirty word 'unsportsmanlike' long before the Post Office got its claws on it. Bill Jeanes, the South Australian secretary of the Board of Control, was using our room more or less as his office as the famous message was being concocted. If anybody in our room thought that the obnoxious term was inappropriate to the occasion he certainly refrained from saying so. For my part I thought that the cable fell miles short of putting the Australian case adequately. I certainly agreed with 'unsportsmanlike'. I still do, and have never missed an opportunity to say so. Had a plebiscite been taken in our dressing room as to the wisdom of using that particular word the result would have been twelve-nil in favour. Had it gone to the same vote right around Australia the odds in its favour would have been astronomical.

Contrary to popular opinion, from the day of that first cable all the real drama of that series departed the scene. The fire seemed to go out. All that remained were the obsequies and, of course, the collecting of whatever loot there was to be dropped into cricket's hat from the pockets of cricket enthusiasts who could still stand the sight of it.

As a player, plugging along after our Board had dipped their flag to the MCC, who made an almost barbarous reply to that opening cable, I thought that in keeping going I was doing nothing more than living a lie. I knew in my heart that the MCC had assumed the righteous attitude of a worthless headmaster dealing with a school scene about which he had taken not the slightest trouble to become conversant. All the talk that has gone on since about those events leaves me completely cold. I laugh scornfully when someone occasionally comes up with the suggestion that Prime Ministers, Ambassadors, even the Royal Court became involved in the shindy. If they did it would have been nothing more than a few muttered inanities expressed over the enticing rim of a tinkling glass at a cocktail party.

It did not for a moment offer shattering threats to the Empire, as has been so often suggested. Common sense amongst the players on both sides took all that silly nonsense out of the show as soon as we resumed hostilities in the fourth Test in Brisbane.

Indeed by the time the fifth Test came around Harold Larwood, who went in as night-watchman and stayed to bat beautifully the next day, was cheered to the echo by crowd and players alike as he left the SCG after making 98. Everyone would have liked to see him get his century–provided of course that he got out immediately afterwards.

If criticism has to be levelled at anybody apart from Douglas Jardine, who later became a firm friend of many Australian cricketers, it would certainly have to be levelled at Pelham Warner. Plum should have chosen a more tactful time to barge into the Australian dressing room than that Saturday afternoon when the heat was on. And, when he settled in again to write his column for the London *Daily Telegraph*, it would have been much wiser had he not made the thoughtless remark that Jack Fingleton was responsible for releasing the story of Woodfull's reply to the world at large. That was an unpardonable mistake.

It was not possible that such a hot story could be kept undercover for more than a few hours. As it was it remained undercover, so far as the general press was concerned, for over a day. Warner came into our dressing room during the Saturday afternoon. The cricket writers, a large team from all the Australian newspapers, had spent the Sunday being entertained right royally at Seppelt's Winery in the Barossa Valley. A journalist from Sydney, Claude Corbett, who had remained for the day in Adelaide, told them of Woodfull's remark when they returned to their hotel in the late evening. Claude had already sent his story through to Sydney as a scoop, but probably thought it such a thunderously hot one that it should be parcelled out immediately to his fellows.

As for who got the story out of the Australian dressing room – that's beside the point. Woodfull made the remark, and we all agreed with him. Only one side *was* playing cricket. The game which Douglas Jardine was presiding over and which was defended so stoutly by the moguls of the MCC had nothing to do with the game we had been brought up to play.

In Brisbane, the fourth Test, Woodfull carried on from his inspired 73 not out in Adelaide, to get 67 in partnership with Victor Richardson who scored a brilliant 83 before Don Bradman contributed 76, his second best performance of the series. England had no real trouble in dealing with our impoverished attack – Grimmett had been dropped – although they did have to drag little Eddie Paynter from his hospital bed when 6 first innings wickets had fallen for 216 runs. Eddie made a gallant 83 in Brisbane's tropical heat, the thermometer scored a century before lunch, and my 51-year-old bowling mate Dainty Ironmonger and I delivered 111 of the 176 Australian overs bowled.

We had England well and truly on the run before Douglas sent his equerries routing around the hospital wards looking for Paynter. Douglas himself knew it and, without any disrespect to Dainty Ironmonger, I still believe that we would have won that game if Grimmett had been on hand to polish off the tailenders, Allen, Larwood and Verity, who gave Paynter such priceless support. That's one of the 'ifs' that make every sportsman's life such a wonderful fantasy land.

From Brisbane to the final Test in Sydney, which took on the semblance of the last night of a show that had died on its feet. Sydney enthusiasts, who had flown to their seventh heaven a few months before when Stan McCabe had pulverized the English attack, treated it as though it were a Club game.

Richardson collected a pair, 'Purka' Lee, the South Australian off spinning all-rounder, made a splendid debut in Tests, and Len Darling, the aggressive Victorian left-hander, made such a great impression that he became an automatic choice for the 1934 tour of England.

13 Sticks and Stones

That bodyline season provided so many warnings to the cricket world that posterity, in deliberations yet to come, will find itself harking back to the fact that some blatant examples of ill-informed and weak-kneed administration on both sides of the world–especially so in the northern hemisphere–left behind a legacy of trouble. The problems have not yet been properly resolved.

Why did England refuse to recognize bodyline as the menace that it was? To me, the answer is easy. They curled up within their shell at the use of the word 'unsportsmanlike'. They couldn't stomach that. But it *was* unsportsmanlike, and I am sure that their unpardonable reluctance to look the thing fair in the face has led to the proliferation of bouncers which have taken so much of the finesse out of the game, and so much of the enjoyment out of the pleasurable pastime of watching cricket.

I have yet to meet one knowledgeable cricket watcher prepared to admit that he enjoys watching three or four fast bowlers plugging away day-long. One does not use the word 'pleasure' when faced with the prospect of watching a succession of overs delivered by men who run in from the vicinity of the sightboards and whack the ball down short, hoping to scare the resistance out of a batsman loaded down with a weight of armour that would have immoblized the legendary Richard Coeur de Lion.

It is all so preposterously ridiculous that one would laugh

uproariously as the stupid scene unfolded, if it wasn't such a tragedy. Yet it could have been avoided. Here in Australia the bouncer became taboo right up until the resumption of cricket after the Second World War. A bowler was regarded as a social leper if he appeared to let one go with malice aforethought. Should he exasperatedly let one fly, he was always very quick to say, 'Sorry, it slipped.'

Tacitly, Australia had quite obviously clamped down on the bowling head-hunter. England curiously refrained from doing so, and they were in charge of the rule book. Why did they not act to outlaw persistent bouncers? Easy again. Their pride had been hurt. Australians however, who had been through the bodyline mill, thought it much easier to suffer a blow to the pride than to the head. Sticks and stones will break your bones . . .

To put things in their modern perspective – perhaps to soothe English feelings – it is fitting to state here and now that Australian bowlers have exploited the bouncer ad infinitum during the past fifteen years, and many Australians, administrators included, have presided over the melancholy scene with glee. Probably, when it comes to the showdown, we Australians can plead the right of retaliation.

Before many years go by cricket will eliminate the bouncer delivered with malice. It should have been rubbed right off the slate in 1933. England then was offended by the use of one word, and the Australian cricket hierarchy fell to its knees in supplication, fearing that in pursuing their threat to take the bat and ball and go home to Mummy, they would ruin their hopes of record gate takings. The aroma of it still persists.

Larwood was a truly great bowler, and his success with the short-pitched ball was outstanding, but by the time the campaign came to its conclusion in Sydney, where England drew down the curtains with an eight wickets' victory, Larwood had bowled himself into the ground. Jardine had used him ruthlessly in his campaign to subdue the batting genius of Don Bradman, and he succeeded, probably beyond his wildest dreams. Bradman scored a fine century in Melbourne, and his last four Test innings were 76, 24, 48 and

71, but bodyline wore him down. Every Australian knew full well that Bradman's domination, seen in 1930, had taken leave, except perhaps in the Melbourne innings, where he had the benefit of the slowest pitch of the season. Not once in that eventful Test season did he bat with anything like the domination expected of him. It would be an insult to Bradman's unique ability to say that he was not seriously rattled by the bodyline tactics. Only once however did the English bouncer barrage succeed in landing a blow on him. That 'success' came to them in the fifth Test, when the champion collected one on his left forearm.

Every Australian batsman apart from Bradman collected so many bruising blows that Bradman's miraculous ability to keep his hit-score down to one has come to be regarded as a sure sign of his ingenuity in evolving a batting tactic beyond the ability of his team-mates. That he had such ability is not in doubt, but he had to sacrifice his normal technique and outlook in dealing with Larwood. He had to dart from side to side, play reckless shots, and rely on making contact with the bat if the ball was not where he had anticipated. As a result he was frequently beaten, and sometimes made to look second-rate.

I should add at this stage that, making full use of my captain's orders, I made absolutely certain that no one landed a blow on me during the season.

McCabe's 187 in the first Test goes down with me as the finest innings I have seen – no other comes close to it. It was an inspiration to every proud Australian who was lucky enough to see it, to hear it, or to read about it. With the deck and the odds stacked threateningly against him, he proceeded to lay waste, even sack, England's cricket might. That innings will be recalled with pride as long as this country of ours continues to love and enjoy the game of cricket.

As for the magnificent Woodfull, his courage remains an imperishable memory with me. I resent the fact that public appreciation of his wonderful contribution to Australia's presence in that woeful series is being allowed to dip over memory's horizon, as other much less inspiring incidents are recalled and discussed ad nauseam.

Australia would have retaliated in that 'bouncer war', let there be not the slightest doubt, had any other than the highly conscionable William Maldon Woodfull been leading the opposition. Many times it has been said that Australia had no chance of retaliating, that we didn't have the bowlers capable of bowling fast enough. Such talk is nonsense. Do not listen to it.

Woodfull, from the soles of his trustworthy batting boots, believed that the tactic was a totally unworthy one. Nothing, nobody, could have persuaded him to give it a go by setting up his own packed leg field. That is why Australia did not retaliate. Perhaps that is also why there were obvious second thoughts about his leadership when the announcement of his appointment as captain was so shamefully delayed for the Melbourne Test.

Apart from the men I have mentioned – Bradman, McCabe and Woodfull – I believe that I came high on the Australian list of successful performers with 27 Test wickets from 383 eight-ball overs which yielded 724 runs. Yet I got very little pleasure from the series, apart from the warming feeling of having survived enormous pressure in the company of eighteen other Australians who like me were glad when the hostilities ceased.

I have to admit that as I filed into our Sydney Cricket Ground dressing room on Tuesday 28 February 1933, Test cricket had lost all its appeal. Indeed I felt that I could not care less whether I ever turned out again for Australia against England, and the thought occurred to me that it was a matter for some serious discussion whether there were any Englishmen worth playing against.

Cricket was a game from which it was easy for me to find all the fun I required in the Saturday afternoon competition, interlaced with the wonderful camaraderie which went hand in hand with occasional weekend cricket trips to the bush.

It became my firm conviction that, should I continue in the national side, I would spare no effort to get all my pleasure from meeting interesting people and admiring memorable places in the company of my treasured team-mates.

My social contacts with that English team of 1932-33 were few and far between. My first conversation with Douglas Jardine was both memorable and surprising. Walking onto the little verandah outside our Brisbane dressing room at the 'Gabba, I came face to face with the English captain, draped in a big bath towel, closely observing the tactics of the 'Gabba's expert groundsman Jack Farquhar, putting his pitch to bed for the night. With a precarious left-handed grip on his bath towel, Jardine shaded his eyes with his right hand as he watched the short strips of tarpaulin being placed in their stipulated positions.

In the closing stages of that day's play the English skipper, opening the innings with Herbert Sutcliffe, had taken more than ninety minutes to score one run. Facetiously I congratulated him with, 'Well batted, Douglas.' Looking straight into my eyes he said, 'Really, Bill, really. Don't you think I was like an old maid defending her virginity?'

With my sails windless my reply was, 'Sorry, Douglas, I am too short in experience to answer that question.'

Those few words represented the bulk of the communication that went on between us outside 'the shop' throughout that long mirthless summer, although he had a word or two to say to me in a businesslike strain the first time we met on the field at the Sydney Cricket Ground in the New South Wales match. Batting at number seven, Jardine applied his 'temperament test' for a new bowler: he told me that I must not follow through along the pitch, thereby damaging its surface.

My reply was brusquely courteous. 'If that's a complaint I advise you to address it to the umpire.' This evidently persuaded Jardine that further pursuit of the tactic would have little effect upon my attitude towards my job.

Such a ploy is often used to advantage against young contestants starting nervously. When Harry 'Bull' Alexander was selected to do the fast bowling in the fifth Test, after Wall had broken down in the fourth, Jardine had certainly done his homework. Having discovered that Bull had often been embarrassed in Sheffield Shield games by complaints about his following through along the pitch, Jardine was quick to have a go at him. Opening the innings, he complained immediately. George Hele spoke to the Victorian fast bowler twice. Having landed his second warning Alexander said, 'I'll bowl round the wicket.' This meant that the ball would come dangerously across the batsman's body as it made its way towards the slips field. Jardine drew the line at that, of course, and he was quick to say, 'No, Harry, all I was asking was that you should take care with your follow through. I didn't want you to change your style.'

'Round the bloody wicket,' was Alexander's reply.

Expectedly, Jardine received an awful smack on his skinny left hip a few moments later. To his great credit, he took it without the slightest demonstration of pain. He walked round his stumps a few times like a horse with stringhalt, and he raised his eyes skyward in supplication, but this brave show was for me the most impressive thing that Jardine did throughout the tour, and I know that many of my team-mates were similarly impressed. We were all, to a man, appreciative of the fact that he himself had at last copped one, and that he could take it as well as dish it out. Later that day Maurice Leyland told me that the blow had brought blood from the hip.

Another night in Brisbane, as I crossed the foyer of the old Bellevue Hotel, I encountered Douglas making his way to the dining room where his team was having their accustomed Saturday evening communal dinner. He invited me to join in, and I hurriedly accepted, regarding it as an opportunity to extend my examination of this unusual Cromwellian personality. Douglas sat at the head of the table with fourteen-year-old Mary Maguire, the youngest daughter of the Bellevue's proprietor.

I enjoyed the night, but not nearly so much as I did Jardine's dinner in the Masters' rooms at Trinity College, Oxford, when he was my friendly agreeable host some twenty years later.

In those later years, when I came into close association with him per favour of the *Sydney Morning Herald* and cricket's Press Boxes, I was overjoyed to find that Douglas Jardine was human, even shyish. I was thunderstruck. Surely this was not the same bloke I knew in Australia in the summer of 1932-33. It looked like him: long, angular and forbidding. The conformation and the colour of the face, the high cheek bones and long pointed nose of America's

Hiawatha were just as much in evidence. Yet there had been a strange but moving change. I liked him, and I told him so.

I am very glad I met the Jardine of the Press Box. He is never likely to be forgotten in cricket's history, for a reason diametrically opposite to the one which I hold pleasantly in my memory of him now.

14 Credit Where It's Due

Having emerged safely from the bodyline campaign, my best friends were quick to applaud my decision to marry my beloved Molly Herbert, and to disappear from public notice in the backwater that was Kogarah Intermediate Boys' High School. They all reckoned that a young man who had shown that he could survive the trials and tribulations of scone theory should be a very safe bet to survive a matrimonial engagement. They were right. Molly O'Reilly and I have already had over fifty years of happy navigation on that untroubled sea.

My father-in-law, Richard Herbert of Longford, County Meath, joined the New South Wales police in 1886 and apart from a term spent along the Darling River in the 1890s, when shearers' strikes demanded close attention, he spent all his working life in Sydney. His wife, Kate Beston, was from County Clare, and together they spent their married life in Windsor Street, Paddington, where I was lucky to meet their sixth child, Mary Agnes, in 1932.

We married on 6 May 1933, in St Francis Xaviers' Church in Oxford Street, Paddington. Our first home was in Hudson Street, Hurstville, where a boyish Ray Lindwall came once or twice a week to perform in kerosene tin cricket matches in the middle of the street.

Our daughter, Patricia Mary Doherty was born on 9 November 1934, two days after my return from my first overseas tour, to

England in 1934. Then came the Australian cricket tour to South Africa in the 1935-36 season. Our son Peter William had to wait until 18 February 1937 to join the team.

Our marriage has easily withstood the thin ice of the many separations caused by cricket tours as a player, then as a journalist – five to England, and one each to South Africa and New Zealand – as well as the hurly-burly of constant travel around Australia. For that the credit must go without the slightest doubt to that unwavering loyalist, Molly O'Reilly.

If, gentle reader, in the remainder of this autobiography-like tome you should notice that not much mention is made of my family life, the reason is that it has been unexceptional, except perhaps that it has always been exceptionally happy. We have six grandchildren – three boys and three girls, four O'Reillys and two Dohertys – of whom we are extremely proud. Four of them are redheads, just to prove that the Hibernian strain is still around.

They are aware that their old grandfather made a bit of a name for himself a long while ago, but all of them are making their way ahead in the world quite independently of the game of cricket.

15 Liquid Refreshment

Any self-respecting bowler who loses gallons of perspiration during a day's work out in the middle finds out quickly enough that the liquid replacement process must go on, and that there is no better nor more pleasant way of doing it than to sit down at the end of play for a few quiet beers. The first never touches the sides as the saying goes, it just goes up in steam.

When I first played Test cricket for Australia in a full-scale series I set out with the idea of concentrating fully on physical fitness so that I could carry out responsibly the tough job that lay ahead of me. Misguidedly, I thought the best way to do so was to cut out beer drinking altogether and to get to bed quickly enough to get a good night's sleep. I was kidding myself.

I lost nine pounds (4 kg) during the Sydney Test which began the series, and I discovered that consequent painful cramps disturbed my sleep. As a result it became my habit to go through the whole programme all over again in my sleep. The Lord only knows how many wickets I got that season, day and night, but I know that there were very many more than were shown in the scorebooks.

To show how far I was prepared to go with my keep fit policy, I remember alighting from the Melbourne express en route to the south one hot morning, along with Stan McCabe and Victor Richardson, who suggested that we should breast the bar and shout ourselves a cold beer. When I ordered an orange juice I created such a stir that I counted myself lucky that my two companions finally agreed to sink their dignity and remain with me. Even the ragging that followed me around Australia did not shame me out of my determined policy. It was not until I reached Brisbane for the fourth Test that the scheme went wrong.

There, our bowling brigade was woefully depleted by the inexcusable omission of Clarrie Grimmett, who was in fact the best bowler on either side. Australia took the field with three recognized bowlers, Tim Wall, Bert Ironmonger and myself.

The thermometer on the scale used in those days, invented by Mr Fahrenheit, went just above the century mark. In Brisbane's sub-tropical humidity such a day was enough to try the staying power of anyone doing a tough physical job. Wall's heel bruised quickly on the concrete-like pitch, which left Ironmonger and me carrying the baby.

Dainty Ironmonger, my fellow galley slave, was getting ready to celebrate his fifty-first birthday. He was a heavily built man, fifteen-and-a-half stone and six feet high, and those of us who looked closely when he was preparing for the fray knew that he wore long pieces of rubber band about six inches wide wrapped firmly round each thigh. I had no idea what benefit they gave him. Besides this, Dainty pulled an elastic knee guard over each knee, wore two pairs of woollen socks, and thrust his feet into boots with soles an inch thick.

On that day I write about in Brisbane, I honestly believe he deserved the Victoria Cross. When he had bowled about ten overs I met him as we were changing over and I can recall the tortured look in his eye as he enquired what my reaction to the pitch was. Dainty was still going at the end of the day, and in doing the job he did he won my complete admiration and everlasting affection.

I bring this into the story not only to pay a genuine tribute to my brave old partner, but to give you some idea of the way I felt as I walked off the field at the end of the day. At the pavilion gate I was drawn aside by a friend, Dr Stan McDonnell of St George in southwestern Queensland, who said, 'I'd like to have a few words with you, Tiger.'

He told me he was worried about me, that he had watched me bowl all the way round Australia that season, and that he suspected I was completely washed out. I believed him. As he pushed me towards the dressing room he said, 'I'll be waiting for you when you come out, and then I shall prescribe.'

The only interest I had in the dressing room was in finding an uncluttered seat where I could stretch out and lie, or die, in peace. Dainty, with the same purpose in mind had already found his retreat on the far side of the room. When our team-mates started to worry about us remaining in our sopping wet gear and resisting all their efforts to get us moving towards the shower room, Stan McCabe approached Bill Woodfull with the suggestion that a glass of champagne might get his two bowlers back on their feet. Bill of course would never have thought of it, he was a dedicated teetotaller, but he reacted quickly and asked our room attendant, Sid Redgrave, to go to the bar and bring back a cold bottle of Great Western, and charge it to the Board of Control.

Sid returned red-faced to say that the big cricket boss in Brisbane, barrister Jack Hutcheon, a Queensland representative on the Australian Board of Control, had countermanded the skipper's order by forbidding the drink to be served. Woodfull, furious, put his blazer on and went out again with Redgrave. They returned with the champagne. I never heard what went on outside the room, but I do know that neither our captain nor Redgrave paid for the medicine prescribed by Dr McCabe. It worked well enough for me to go to work in the shower room and to meet Stan McDonnell in due course. As he drove me to the Jonsonian Club in Adelaide Street, he spoke learnedly about the manner in which one's body reacted to an abnormal loss of moisture. His emphasis on loss of weight, crippling cramps, and disturbed sleep was so realistic that I was prepared and eager to act upon his expert advice. He led me straight to the bar and, not even pausing to enter my name in the Visitors' Book, ordered a pint of Four X served in a tankard taken straight from the refrigerator. As soon as I had dealt hurriedly and gratefully with that, he had another just the same waiting on the counter.

When I was in a fit condition to relax and listen carefully, he told me that it was a very dangerous procedure not to take steps to replace lost body moisture and that I must never again attempt such a dangerous programme as I had set myself that important season.

Stan's point, God bless him, was well and truly taken.

Two years later in South Africa I ran across a similar situation. Our team, Victor Richardson's 1935-36 Australian touring side, was invited to go down a goldmine on the Rand. They had already bored it down past the five thousand feet level. Nearly a mile underground, we were not happily impressed with the heat and the humidity, and had had quite enough of the conditions within the hour. We were delighted to get back to the minehead where we were taken to inspect the company's takings for the previous day. Resting on a table in a back room of the office was a golden brick, about regulation size, and the mine boss informed us that any one of us who could lift the brick one-handed was free to wrap it up and take it back to Australia.

Back to the loss of body moisture: we were shown the room in which each mine worker was weighed at change of shift, and his loss of weight recorded. Every man was given a copious drink of water dashed with glucose, and ordered to sit comfortably in the medical room until he had completely relaxed, and had returned to his normal weight. Those black miners were too valuable to their mining industry not to pay careful attention to their state of health.

I bring this treatise to a close by offering my sympathy and compassion to every hard-working Englishman who finds that a loss of moisture problem worries him. I cannot in sympathy advise him to cure himself with an enjoyable, therapeutic beer. English beer is generally delivered to its victims so hot – not warm, hot – that they must necessarily fan it with their bats to cool it down so it won't burn the lips. That's how it was in my day. Perhaps things have changed for the better. As I tried to pretend that I could handle their beer in England, I used to wonder how they had produced great men like Robin Hood, Harold Larwood and Bill Voce, all of Nottinghamshire, on the lifeless concoction which went under the same four letter word as our own.

16 Injury to Insult

The 1933-34 season began perilously for me. I had felt that my growing cricket ambition was sure to be realized when the Australian selectors nominated their team to tour England in 1934. By leading the Test wicket-takers in the series against England the previous summer, I knew that my invitation to tour was sure to come provided I kept fit. That nearly didn't happen.

Wendell Bill, an opening bat for the Waverley club in Sydney and for New South Wales, and incidentally one who always came into consideration for the national side, invited me to join a team he was taking to Tumut, in the mountains in southern New South Wales. Such matches have always been popular with first-class players as they afford a splendid opportunity to get in some valuable match practice before the real season begins. They also give Sydney players the chance to experience the brand of magnificent hospitality for which rural New South Wales cricket has always been famous. I jumped at the chance. Not only did it fulfill all the above requirements, it also led me to look forward to renewing friendships with many Tumut lads who had been contemporaries of mine at St Pats in Goulburn.

We played on a concrete pitch with a coir matting cover, and I shall take this opportunity to pay my respects to those matting wickets. They did me enormous favours. Medium paced spinning was really made to order for coir mats. I could turn the ball quite noticeably, and coming from my height of six feet three inches the ball could be relied upon to lift disconcertingly from a good length. It was difficult for a batsman to keep the ball down unless he could manage to hit straight through the half-volley.

The approach to the delivery crease was the only thing the Tumut committee had failed to organize for their big game. Large holes loomed as hazards to bowler's safety on the delivery stride, and late on the Sunday afternoon I carelessly stomped my left foot into one which was big enough to accommodate a young wombat. The resultant pulled intercostal muscle (between the ribs) concerned me ceaselessly over the next month.

I continued to appear for North Sydney's first grade side, not telling anyone about my problem – a policy I suppose springing from the old axiom 'least said soonest mended' – but despite many trips to Tom Langridge, who used to have a clinic and gymnasium near Circular Quay in Sydney, I had begun to think that the damaged rib muscle was threatening to obliterate all my ideas of a trip to England in March 1934.

It disappeared just as quickly as it came. Lining up to bowl against Western Suburbs for North Sydney, skippered by Don Bradman who had left St George to join us, I decided to start the day with a rip-roaring 'quicky'. Going well back, I galloped through like Phar Lap and gave that delivery everything I could – arm, body and follow through. I never felt the pain again. For some mysterious reason it had gone completely and I showed my grateful appreciation to whomever was responsible by collecting four wickets with four successive balls later that afternoon.

My recovery from the injury sustained at Tumut quickly showed up in the Sheffield Shield season which started in November. In Brisbane I collected 13 wickets for 111 runs. In that game Bradman scored 200 in 184 minutes and with Bill Brown put on 294 runs in less than three hours. Brown's century did a lot for his chances of going to England.

A month later in Adelaide my stocks slumped heavily, when I failed to get a wicket whilst South Australia put together over 300 runs. My failure to get wickets in Adelaide weighed just as heavily on my mind as it did in the pen and ink of several exinternationals, who reckoned that I was performing like a spent volcano. The Adelaide pitch never thrilled me at any stage of my career. I used to say that it had been laid out by an undertaker, it never had the slightest show of life in it. Clarrie Grimmett used to laugh when I spoke in that strain, and would simply ask me to take a look at his performances for South Australia. That advice never profited me much, but you can take it from me that Adelaide in those days was a graveyard for any bowler who hoped to get some advantage from speed off the pitch.

A week later my confidence returned at the Melbourne Cricket Ground, where I collected 9 wickets for 50 runs in Victoria's second innings, giving me 12 wickets for the match. That was my bowling swan song for the season. Realizing I suppose that I'd had an extra heavy season the previous year, when I had been asked to carry the major Australian bowling responsibilities, and that I was likely to be just as busy in England right through the Australian winter of 1934, the New South Wales selectors, mainly through the advice of my respected friend Chappie Dwyer, the chairman of the NSW selection committee, decided to taper off the effort required of me for the remainder of the 1933-34 season. With 33 Shield wickets, 25 of them from two matches, I finished at the head of the State averages and felt that things had gone well enough for me to start making arrangements about the leave required for a March to November absence from my job.

There were few surprises in the team chosen to go to England in 1934, but Jack Fingleton's absence stunned me. No argument was strong enough to convince me that he should not have been one of the first men chosen. His performances against Larwood, Voce, Allen and Verity in the bodyline season had won him immortality as an opening batsman of great determination and courage. He was a thoroughly dedicated performer prepared to give all that he had to offer at any stage of a game. I knew him very well both on and off the field, and I knew that the Australian team would not be nearly as strong without him. Deeply as I regretted his omission, Fingleton himself was affected even more. He had set his whole life on making that trip, it was his life's ambition. Eighteen months later he was destined to tour South

Africa, where he covered himself with glory in a succession of batting performances that have rarely been excelled, but the shine went out of his eyes when he missed that 1934 trip. That was the first time I had real cause to doubt the sanity of the men whose duty it was to pick the very best team available on every occasion. There have been many doubts since.

The one man in that 1934 side who must have bought himself a ticket or two in Tatts when he heard the announcement was the late Ernie Bromley, a Western Australian playing for Victoria, who at twenty-one was the baby of the side. He was chosen on the strength of a long Melbourne innings against South Australia in which he had handled Grimmett's bowling fairly responsibly. That of course was an excellent test. In the final engagement before the touring team was chosen Bromley had scored 92 against us in Sydney, but he was very lucky there and his luck came at the best possible time for him. Before he had opened his score he was missed off successive balls from me by Bertie Oldfield behind stumps. Oldfield seldom missed anything. For him to miss two in a row was unthinkable. Bromley was a magnificent fieldsman. He threw the ball 125 yards in a competition one day at the MCG and he was said to be a useful left-arm bowler. Unfortunately, as it turned out on tour, his bowling ability was mainly in the minds of the selectors.

The team comprised seven New South Welshmen: Bradman, McCabe, Kippax, Brown, Chipperfield, O'Reilly and Oldfield, and seven Victorians: Ponsford, Woodfull, Barnett, Darling, Bromley, Ebeling and Fleetwood-Smith. Grimmett and Wall from South Australia completed the quota of sixteen. Perhaps the jealousy which is supposed to underlie everything in which New South Wales and Victoria compete had something to do with the last minute inclusion of Ernie Bromley in preference to Jack Fingleton. Seven from each state was a nice even position.

Perhaps another incident had something to do with it. Fingleton had scored a splendid 145 in the vital match in Sydney where Billy Brown had made his trip secure with a long capable innings of 205. When Fingleton's score stood at 86 he played a ball from Ebeling to second slip, where it was fielded. Fingleton then went forward along the pitch to do some of his customary gardening. With Fingleton out of his crease repairing the wicket, second slip returned to 'keeper Barnett who removed the bails. On appeal, umpire George Borwick, one of the two leading umpires, gave the decision 'out', assuming, I suppose rightfully enough, that the ball was not dead when Fingleton left his wicket unattended.

Bill Woodfull, Victoria's captain, righted the situation. He had a hurried word or two with Borwick then rushed out to lay his hand on Fingleton's shoulder and steer him back towards the wicket which he had just left in high dudgeon. For a moment it looked to me as though Fingo was going to refuse Woodfull's invitation to return. It is easy to imagine just how he felt about the dismissal which had shortened his opportunity to make the most of this last vital opportunity to assure himself of his England tour. He did return to make another 59, but it struck me that this affair might have cost Fingleton his trip. His reluctance to seize Woodfull's hospitality wholeheartedly may have been construed quite wrongly by people in executive cricket positions.

Fingleton himself had other ideas about his omission: he believed that a newspaper article from the pen of Don Bradman had not been helpful. As I recall, Bradman had been critical of Fingleton's running between wickets—perhaps with some justification. Fingleton had a bad habit of taking a few quick paces down the wicket after he played a shot, as if he were going to run, but then stopping. He occasionally left his batting partner stranded.

Whatever the cause of his omission, from that time onward I noticed a streak of deep resentment in his make-up, for which I have remained ever since sympathetically saddened. That resentment accompanied Fingleton throughout his long and useful life as a top-line journalist in cricket and in the political sphere, and though he tried hard to curb its influence, there were times when he couldn't keep it in check, and he let it boil over.

Had he lived long enough to find himself branded a liar one can imagine the spontaneity of his vigorous reaction. That branding took place in the recent publication *Bradman—The Illustrated Biography* in which Michael Page charges that Fingleton's denial, in his autobiography *Batting from Memory*, that he was the player who gave the press the story of Woodfull's famous remark to Pelham Warner during the bodyline tour, was a lie.

Realizing that Michael Page was twelve when the incidents took place, and that at the time he was living twelve thousand miles away in his native England, I am inclined to take Page's allegations with a grain of salt, and do not wish to dwell on a topic that would have been better left to lie in its proper place under the floor coverings. However from my first-hand experience of Fingleton, formed over fifty years of sport, business and social friendship, never did I get the slightest impression that he was a liar. He was not.

I must add on Jack Fingleton's behalf that I was present at a pre-breakfast natter at an hotel in Hastings in 1948 when Sir Pelham Warner, 'Old Plum' as we called him, joined Fingleton and me before we walked in for our meagre serving of bacon and egg – singular if you please, rationing was still rife. When Plum appeared I felt the air electrify. I knew that this was an opportunity that Fingleton could not possibly resist. He had only recently written *Cricket Crisis*, which is still recognized as the best exposé of the bodyline tour, and was then hailed with glowing admiration by top-line cricket writers like Neville Cardus, R C Robertson-Glasgow and Ian Peebles. In the book he had taken Sir Pelham to task for having stated that Fingleton had released the story of Woodfull's remarks to the English manager.

My feeling of discomfiture was accentuated as soon as the old man placed his bottom on the cane chair. 'Good morning, Sir Pelham,' Fingo began. 'Top of the morning to you. I have been waiting a long time for an opportunity to ask whether you still think that I was the culprit who leaked the story about your famous conference with Woodfull in Adelaide.'

Those forthright words were typical of Fingleton's approach. Warner replied immediately, 'Indeed no, Jack. I have reason to believe now that in my first hasty reaction when I wrote that you were the prime candidate for the disclosure I was wrong. I am sorry and I apologize.' That was all. We marched off into the breakfast room and the subject was not resurrected in our breakfast conversation. Perhaps Plum was too hungry to go on with it.

That put an end to the matter so far as I was concerned.

17 Five Weeks at Sea

I have said before that the bodyline series destroyed my youthful notions of Test cricket and that the prospect of playing against England again was not a pleasant one for me. Fortunately the time soon came when my critical opinions of English cricket and cricketers, forged in the heat of that awful summer, were blown to smithereens by the wonderful events of 1934, my first trip to the United Kingdom.

We left for England in March. The team congregated in Melbourne, where we were given the accustomed words of farewell, the shrewd words of warning about conducting ourselves in the manner fitting to the ambassadorial roles we were about to play, and above all a stern diatribe on keeping our mouths absolutely shut on any topic that looked like culminating in a discussion of the taboo subject–bodyline.

Our first port of call was Launceston where we played a match against Tasmania and picked up Harold Bushby, a Launceston-based barrister and a member of the Australian Board of Cricket Control. Bushby had fortuitously gained selection as tour manager when New South Wales and Victoria quarrelled over the job and each had voted for the Tasmanian representative.

Two things stand out very clearly in my mind about that first game of the tour. Firstly, I was named as twelfth man for the first time in my life. I shared the job with my mate Hans Ebeling who, like me, was stunned to find that no dressing-room beer was provided by the local Cricket Association despite the depressing heat of a day which made the going hard out in the field. Harold Bushby started off on the wrong foot by telling us that no beer would be consumed in the dressing room whilst he was manager. Undaunted, we bought a dozen Cascade from the bar, borrowed a tub from the dining room, filled it with ice, and were able to welcome the team back convivially at the end of the day. We were never reimbursed for the cost of the beer.

The other memory is of Chuck Fleetwood-Smith spinning the ball so prodigiously in the nets before the game began that both Len Darling and Bill Woodfull told him to shove off whilst they tried to get some proper practice.

We played another game in Hobart and one at Perth, then we set out on the long sea voyage.

It is not easy to describe the wonderful experience it is for a jaded cricketer, wearied with a hard season's unrelenting effort directed towards attaining the consummate goal of a tour of England, to find himself faced with the entrancing prospect of five weeks at sea. Waking each morning to the realization that breakfast in bed is available before attempting the onerous job of shaving and indulging in a warm sea-water bath. Then the task of filling in a long hot day lolling about in deck chairs on the sports deck, engaging in the various deck games that you are unable to talk your way out of, talking to bevies of beautiful girls, eating your very head off, drinking much more icy beer than is good for your liver in tropical climes, and generally acting like an indolent layabout who has no excuse to offer for his worthless outlook on life.

It was heaven to us all – well, most of us. There could not possibly, we thought, ever have been a better life invented. Even ancient Ulysses who spent those legendary years sailing about the sunny Mediterranean trying to make up his mind to go back home to his beloved Penelope could not possibly have had it better than we did. To add to our great happiness prices at the café bar were ridiculously cheap as a result of all excise duties having been thrown overboard as soon as our ship, the RMS *Orford*, Orient liner, left the Australian port of Fremantle.

The ship's menus were printed daily on the ship's press and were so extensive that one would quickly run out of steam if one attempted to run down the entire litany. Every night there was such a list of amusements that passengers found it irksome to decide whether dancing, cinema, cards, lively conversation or just over-indulgence in the forward lounge was to hold one's attention for the evening. My mouth waters as I write. It is a self-satisfying thought to remember that I enjoyed the whole set-up so thoroughly that I was sorry when it ended.

During this idyllic experience the sixteen of us got to know each other as if we were brothers living under the same roof. Those of us who needed a little brushing up on the social niceties got the required grooming by donning our dress jackets for dinner each night and learning the necessary graces through intelligent observation.

The fancy dress ball night was a memorable affair. Billy Ponsford, one of the shyer members of the side, made a tremendous hit dressed up as the black, bearded male model who used to help Pelaco sell their shirts. There was no need for a nautical Sherlock Holmes to trace Ponny's meanderings during the night: he left a trail of footprints of striking definition. He must have emptied every black boot polish tin in the steward's quarters. For want of inspiration most of us dressed in sheets or flowing materials which were meant to lay claim to desert sheikhdom. I have but one unfortunate memory of the voyage: hurrying to join my sunburnt nomadic tribesmen I tripped on my oversized garment and injured both my wrists as I hit the deck.

How deprived are our present day cricketers who set out for and reach England within twenty-four hours. They sit together in twos or threes and meet the rest of the team as they join those long impatient queues which line up interminably outside the lavatories. The present set-up I am assured comes under the name of progress. The same source tells me that modern man has no time to spare for ship travel. The catch-cry, 'I haven't got the time,' which permeates all the human avenues of this twentieth century, is perhaps the saddest pronouncement that mankind has learned to utter. It makes me sad to hear the holiday-makers hell bent on discovering Europe cannot find the time to travel there by ship. The shipboard life is miles better than the touring. If they went just half way there by ship and then turned round and came straight back they would have had the best holiday there is to offer.

Australian cricketers would be an infinitely better band of competitors in England if they were to make their way there by sea. The trouble is that the airways have so comprehensively sold the idea that time is valuable that they have been able to run the shipping lines off the map. If I were Prime Minister I would immediately decree that all our international travellers should make their next trip by sea.

We were delighted with the welcome given us by the people of Colombo when we sailed into their city, known as the 'Gem of the East'. The aroma of the city wafted pleasantly to us far out to sea, adding to the general charm of the beautiful island now known as Sri Lanka. Then across the Arabian Sea, past Cape Guardafui, the northeastern extremity of the African continent, and into the Red Sea with a call at Aden. From Suez we motored across the desert to Cairo where we visited the museum where lay the relics of the young Tutankhamen, whose collection of burial gear constitutes the finest array of ancient artistry known to man.

On our trip out to Mena House Hotel, on the banks of the Nile on the outskirts of Cairo, we met up with the cast of the English cinema production, *The Camels are Coming*. There we fraternized with Jack Hulbert and Cicely Courtneidge before making the usual trip to the pyramids astride camels. Here I had the chance to bring my love for history to the fore. It was a simple matter to visualize our Australian infantrymen settling down to their short training period in the sands out towards Heliopolis, before they were thrown into their impossible task on the cliffs of Gallipoli on the Sunday morning of 25 April 1915, the first Anzac Day. There too I imagined the French troops filling in their time after Nelson had wrecked their fleet in the Battle of the Nile in 1798, thereby destroying their chances of a quick trip home. Perhaps they consoled themselves with the thought that their discovery of the famous Rosetta Stone would open up thousands of years of human history previously lost to mankind.

The trip across the Mediterranean was a joy: the serenity of it, the vivid blueness of the sea which for centuries had remained the hub of civilization, the feeling of coming face to face with what the human story was all about filled me with wonder. Sailing so close to Crete that we could clearly follow the battlements on the island's high central ranges, I thought of old King Minos and his Minotaur. No wonder Ulysses took so long to return from the Trojan Wars.

We wondered why a famous English poet had said, 'See Naples and die'. Perhaps because the harbour lacks the benefit of a discernibly ebbing and flowing tide. We saw hosts of little boats moving about the harbour picking up the flotsam and jetsam which a tide usually handles free of charge. The Mediterranean, except for the narrow Strait of Gibraltar, is landlocked, consequently it is scarcely affected by the great tides which play such an important part in the lives of other great seaboard cities.

We visited the ruins of Pompeii and Herculaneum, obliterated less than a hundred years after the birth of Christ by an eruption of the magnificently forbidding Mount Vesuvius, in whose shadow they stand. We went ashore at the French Riviera, tried our hands at the gaming tables at Monte Carlo, and had time for a brief look at the French tennis championships. The Australian Davis Cup team – Jack Crawford, Vivian McGrath, Don Turnbull and Adrian Quist – had been our shipmates on the voyage, on the way to conduct their own campaign in Europe.

Time is valuable! Nonsense! That voyage was priceless.

18 England 1934

Then came the end of a perfect holiday when the good ship *Orford* docked at Southampton. We were fit, tanned and eager to resume cricket hostilities. We were the eighteenth Australian team to tour England, if you don't count the 1868 tour by a team of Aborigines under the captaincy of Englishman Charles Lawrence. Not, by the way, that that first Australian team should in any way be discounted: they played 47 matches over five months, winning 14, losing 14 and drawing 19, and they drew substantial crowds and made an enormously favourable impression wherever they went. In fact for years afterwards English cricket enthusiasts found it hard to come to terms with the sight of white Australian cricketers. Even as late as 1934 Australians were still explaining to English acquaintances that they had learned to talk English at their mothers' knees. What proved more difficult to explain was the disappointing fact that Australians had all apparently forgotten how to throw spears and boomerangs. Such novelties were part of the fare supplied by the 1868 team.

Nevertheless, we were given an overpowering reception by the press and radio, who, I feel sure, were thoroughly disappointed that not one of us had a single word to say about bodyline. We were all so tired of the word that we ran for cover whenever it was mentioned. Indeed one of the adventurous London dailies, keen to get an early story, had sent a well known journalist with a poison pen, one Trevor Wignall, to join up as shipmate from Port Said on the Suez Canal. Wignall missed out so badly that he described us as the 'silent, sneering sixteen'. That endearing term of welcome was radioed from London back to us aboard ship.

But on our arrival in London, at Waterloo Station, the Minister of War-cum-President of the Marylebone Cricket Club, Lord Hailsham, led the extended-hands-brigade which left us in no doubt at all that we were welcome guests, and that they were courteously eager to see that we knew it. Even the redoubtable Douglas Jardine was in attendance and similarly inclined to wish us well. We had read beforehand that he intended to play no part whatever in the coming test of strength with us. He too had a writing contract.

We were whisked off to the Hotel Langham at the top of Regent Street, diagonally opposite the then headquarters of the BBC. Ten days of welcomes followed. Barring breakfast we had speeches every time we sat at table. Some of them were memorable affairs. From Ramsay MacDonald, the Prime Minster, down to the humblest London cricket enthusiast, we received convincing evidence that we were not going to be assailed with an overwhelming barrage on bodyline. Everybody took pains not to mention it.

And then the cricket began. It was a long and difficult tour. Grimmett and I had plenty of bowling to do, and Woodfull made sure we got all we needed as he set out to finish off the County games in the shortest possible time. It was long before the time when it became necessary to raise flagging public interest by stage-managing games to bring about exciting finishes.

Woodfull was a realist. He believed that a team took the field with the single-minded purpose of coming off it victoriously as quickly as that result could be engineered. He reckoned that the enthusiast who paid money to look at us in action would get his money's worth by seeing us perform 'fair dinkum'. We all agreed with him wholeheartedly.

Grimmett and I were racing neck and neck with each other with fifty wickets each before the tour was half way through. The early Tests came and went without any real domination noticeable. Australia won the first at Nottingham's Trent Bridge, where I took 11 wickets.

Grimmett and I were great mates bowling in double harness, but we competed unashamedly with each other. We rejoiced in each other's successes, but still tried like blazes to beat the socks off each other. On the last day of that Trent Bridge Test it looked as though Australia would run out of time to dismiss England in the second innings. I bowled the last over before lunch to Les Ames from the River end, and half way through it I got a leg break to bite like a whiting as it raised a telling cloud of dust. Who do you think was the second Australian to notice that delivery? Yes, of course. On the way to the pavilion Clarrie questioned me closely on the location of the spot. He was keen to know whether it was on the stumps, and if so which particular stump. I told him that it was fair on middle and right in the blind spot. I knew I was a goner. Of course Clarrie deserved all the goodies that were on offer. Hadn't he gone close to winning the 1930 series in England off his very own right spinning arm?

Sure enough as we were taking the field after lunch Bill Woodfull came up to me, his head hung low, to say, 'I'm going to put old Grum on at the River end next over, Tiger, and switch you up here to the Pavilion end.' I accepted this without demur. Of course he was doing the right thing. Grimmett was his match-winner tried and true. I was a newcomer. I knew that it hurt him to tell me this, for he never once looked me in the eye as he delivered the news, and that was not his custom, so I just said, 'Righto, Will. That's all right by me.'

In my first over after the change I got one to move so promisingly that poor old Clarrie almost cried in disappointment. I went on to collect 7 last innings wickets and to claim much more than my fair share of adulation for winning the match. Never did I let Grimmett forget, but you can take it from me that there was never any need for him to do any of that type of finessing. He was the most competent bowler I have ever laid eyes upon.

England ran all over us in the second Test at Lord's, where the brilliant orthodox left-hander Hedley Verity caught us on a wet wicket and left us for dead. In getting 15 wickets in one day he became the toast of all England and the pride of his native Yorkshire. That was really the only time that I saw Verity performing at full capacity. He was a complete master of length and direction, and coming down from his full height of six feet one he made the ball come chest-high off the damaged pitch. Right-handed batsmen didn't stand a chance of handling him successfully unless they padded their chests extensively and refrained from using their bats on five or six balls per over. The famous cartoonist Tom Webster decorated the menu we used at the official dinner held at the end of that match with a twisted-tailed kangaroo in tears, explaining his discomposure with the words, 'Yea, Verity! Verity!' We got the message.

Bradman's batting form was causing much disquiet in the Australian camp. He had begun the tour with his usual double century at the Cathedral City of Worcester and had followed it up with a big score at Leicester where, as vice-captain, he led us for the first time on tour. In his next appearance, on the entrancingly beautiful Fenner's Green at Cambridge, a young undergraduate named Davies assured himself of immortality by clean bowling the Australian superstar first ball. That blob, his second in England, seemed to start a 'trot' which was so seldom relieved that we began to despair of him. At Lord's against the MCC he was caught and bowled by Freddie Brown for next to nothing, and at Oxford in an uncharacteristically subdued innings he was out lbw for 37. The English press were quick to seize upon our baffling dilemma and to describe it as a nervous aftermath of the trials and tribulations of the champion's nerve-tingling encounters with Larwood and Voce in Australia.

At Southampton he was out for yet another duck, but we all cheered him to the echo when he cracked it at Lord's next match, crashing together 160 runs out of the 225 scored in his stay of just over two hours. He smacked the stuffing out of the ball with such daring that we all thought that the Test matches could not come quickly enough for us.

In the Nottingham Test he had scraped together 29 and 25 and in the second at Lord's 36 and 13. At Taunton against Somerset the veteran slow left-hander Jack White had him snick one to the 'keeper for 17 and in the following match against Surrey the all-rounder Errol Holmes dismissed him for 37. In the second innings of the Surrey match at the Oval he gave promise for the imminent third Test to be played at Manchester by scoring a confident 61 not out at a critical period. The Old Trafford Test was drawn after England had made 627 in the first innings and we had replied with 491, Bradman contributing 30. These performances were so far below what the cricket world had come to expect that the Australian camp was gearing itself sorrowfully to the dismal fact that his previous match-winning capacities had flown the coop.

It was lucky for us that in the meanwhile Bill Woodfull, Stan McCabe and newcomers Billy Brown, Artie Chipperfield and Len Darling had been chipping in with a string of useful scores that had given us bowlers runs to play with. Brown had scored a remarkable century in the Lord's Test before overnight rain had turned it into a horror stretch, and he had gone well in his first Test, at Nottingham. Lord's was Bill's happy batting ground. He scored a Test century there at his first appearance in 1934 and followed it up with a brilliant undefeated opener's effort of 206 not out in 1938. McCabe, who had scored 170 for once out in the Manchester Test was showing such promising form that it gave us some respite from the gloom of Bradman's bad trot.

From the Manchester Test we went straight to Chesterfield to play Derbyshire. In a dogged innings of 71 Bradman gave some fleeting glimpses of returning confidence, and he followed this up with a splendid century against Yorkshire at Sheffield in which he demonstrated that the industrial smoke of the steel-making town held no difficulties for him. This was tremendously welcome for the very next match was the vital fourth Test, where one side or the other was likely to stamp its claim on the series.

The Test was eventually washed out, but not before it had made its claim on Test history. Bradman and Bill Ponsford, in the partnership which the cricket world had been prophesying for six years, scored a record-breaking 388 for the fourth wicket. Ponsford was finally out when, in playing a pull shot which went to the boundary, he scuffed off the leg bail with his ample posterior.

Their partnership had begun at 3 wickets down for 39. Bill Bowes had struck a sharp blow after England had made only 200, clean bowling Brown for 15 and then accounting for Oldfield, sent in as night-watchman, and then Woodfull, each for a duck.

When Bradman accompanied Ponsford to the middle the next morning, all our eyes were upon him facing the first ball of the day from Bowes. He moved right in behind the ball, which was pitched on the stumps, and smacked it defiantly just wide of mid-on for the best looking, most satisfying boundary we Australians had seen that summer. That shot forced off the toes is unarguably the best shot that cricket has to offer. It may not be the most spectacular—nothing like the full-blooded hook or the spanking cover drive—but what it does to a bowler's morale is beyond description. It cut through our dressing room tension like a warm knife cuts through butter. We reckoned our troubles were over. We could settle down for a day's fun. We even perhaps felt a twinge or two of sympathy for the English bowlers.

Bradman went on to make 304 before Bowes sent his off stump flying, and we had the game won when rain came. The Test was drawn and the series was still square at one match all. But we were confident as we left Headingley, our champion batsman had regained his batting equilibrium, and we looked forward to the deciding fifth Test which would be played to a finish at the Oval in a few weeks' time.

There were about six matches to be played before the decider, and I think perhaps it was decided that it would be foolish to let Bradman run the risk of using up too much of his new found confidence in the intervening games. If that were so then it was a wonderful decision. Just one week before the final Test we were due to play Notts County team on their home ground, Trent Bridge at Nottingham. Notts was the home County of Harold Larwood and Bill Voce and it was skippered by Arthur Carr, who was one of the authorities consulted by Douglas Jardine when he was formulating his bodyline campaign theories after the MCC had named him as their captain. No bowler had bowled sconners at us on the tour so far, but we all viewed our Trent Bridge engagement with a certain amount of suspicion.

We arrived at Victoria Station in Nottingham City about 9 p.m. to be greeted by a large, hostile crowd who hooted loudly and offered insults which, expressed in a broad vernacular, were difficult for us to translate. But they left us in no doubt whatever that they didn't like us, that they wished we had not come amongst them, and that they thought we were all chicken-hearted no-hopers who feared their two famous bowlers. To make sure that we got the message fully they lined the streets all the way down to the Black Boy Hotel where we were to be housed during the match.

It turned out to be a shocker. Carr did not play, and for good measure Larwood himself was missing from the local line-up.

We were intrigued at Larwood's non-appearance, for he had played in more than twenty games in the County competition that season and showed clearly enough that he was perfectly fit to play if he wished to do so. Carr was a pugnacious character, very quick on the draw in the newspaper columns he contributed on cricket, and it was surmised that Larwood's absence was at Carr's request and upon his advice. Bradman fortunately did not play either.

Setting his fully-manned, closed-in leg side field, Bill Voce ripped straight into his job with a fully concentrated intimidatory display of the controversial bowling technique which all Australians had thought to have been effectively banned. Woodfull added substantially to our enormous respect for him by batting throughout our innings and defying Voce's dangerous tactics, and before he returned to our dressing room at the end of our innings, Woodfull, still wearing his pads, carried straight through to the County Club's office in the pavilion to advise the secretary-manager that if he was not prepared to say that Voce would be taking no more part in the game Woodfull himself would immediately instruct his team to return to London that night. Voce did not re-appear. When Notts took the field without him in the second innings the crowd stood and hooted us long and loud.

We went on to win back the Ashes at the Oval in a match which witnessed another record partnership between Bradman and Ponsford. They put on 451 for the second wicket, Bradman making 244. Bill Ponsford scored 266 before he was out, again hitting his own wicket whilst pulling a ball to the mid-wicket boundary, just when we felt that he was well on his way to breaking Bradman's world record Test score of 334.

Very little of the tour was left after that fifth Test victory. We had a wonderful trip to Forres in the Scottish Highlands, close to Ramsay MacDonald's home town of Lassiemouth, to try our luck with the Scotland XI. I had the distinction of opening the Australian batting for the second time in my career, and like the legendary MacDougal, I topped the score with 47.

Summing up my experiences on my first cricket tour of England, I quickly recognized my good fortune in having such a dependable bowling partner as Clarrie Grimmett constantly backing me up so knowledgeably day after day. Grimmett's magnificent support in England in 1934 and later in South Africa in the 1935-36 season stands out clearly as the mainspring of much of my personal success with the ball. Not that he ever had any suggestions to offer as to how I should go about my own bowling job – I cannot remember him ever having a point to make in that direction – but his reliability as a bowler and as a companion in any stressful situation was a constant inspiration which I shall never cease to acclaim as loudly as possible. I took his omission from the side that toured England in 1938, when he was still performing in all his glory, so much to heart that I have never been able to forgive the selection committee which deprived me of such an indispensable ally.

As I surveyed the events of the 1934 tour I was also quick to acknowledge the happy fact that I loved bowling on English wickets. It was a fairly dry summer, but we had an occasional pitch that was affected by rain. The first time I had the privilege of bowling on one such was at Leicester in the second fixture of our itinerary, in which I was so confidently at home that I added 11 wickets for 79 runs to my tally. In those conditions I could get my quickish leg break to grip and turn: I can still recall the surprised look with which Eddie Dawson, the County's right-handed opening batsman, recognized the fact that I had turned sharply from the leg to hit his wicket with a ball which he thought he had well covered. Every time I met Dawson from that day onward he always reminded me that it was the greatest surprise of his cricket career.

At Taunton when we played Somerset late in the tour, we played on a similar pitch and I collected 9 first innings wickets in quick time. I did not have the pleasure of performing on such pitches in the Tests. It would have been the greatest thrill of my bowling life had I been lucky enough to have had a go on that Lord's pitch where Hedley Verity cut us to ribbons. The pitch was dry and hard when England batted, and my contribution was 1 for 70 from 38 overs. In fact I have to accept a lot of the blame for that overwhelming Australian defeat. When I went to bat at number nine, with 8 wickets down for 273 in our first innings, we needed only 17 runs to save the follow on. Arthur Chipperfield was batting confidently at the other end. I had always fancied myself against Verity. I was a left-handed batsman and the ball coming in to me as I stood on the wrong side of the bat never struck fear into my batting heart. All I had to do was hang around patiently whilst my friend Chipperfield knocked off the few required runs. With only 6 runs to go to save the day, success had gone so far to my swollen batting head that I tried to get them in one fell swipe over the closely packed field and into the Lord's Long Room. I had overmatched myself, and the ball got through under my bat to hit the stumps.

It served me right. One moment of wandering in the Elysian fields of batsmanship cost me what could well have been the most rewarding experience of my life on the cricket field. As it was Hedley Verity had the use of the pitch again and took 8 for 43 from 22 overs.

Knowing that the diminutive leg spinner 'Tich' Freeman from Kent continuously showed up as the most prolific wicket-taker in English cricket, it seemed to me that England was the place for me if ever I should decide to play cricket for a living. Freeman, bowling his lofted spinners, was a constant threat to the best batsmen in the land. How much easier it would have been for me, bowling at twice his pace and coming down from a point at least twelve inches higher than Freeman's arm ever reached. I thought that England might be my bowling paradise, especially if I could have coaxed Grimmett to make the experiment with me. During the 1934 Tests Clarrie and I had claimed 53 of the 71 English wickets that fell, and on the tour we each took well over a hundred wickets.

My most rewarding performance of the series was accomplished in the third Test played on Manchester's Old Trafford. Primed with Old Trafford's comforting history of rain-affected pitches, I looked forward to a bit of fun. In that game not a drop of rain fell: Lancashire was hit with an unaccustomed heat wave that kept the St John's ambulance stretcher bearers busy attending the spectators overcome with heat. England's skipper Bob Wyatt won the toss and batted. Cyril Walters and Herbert Sutcliffe were away to a fine start, especially Walters, and had 68 runs on the board when drinks came out at the end of the first hour's play.

With conversation flowing freely as the drinks were dispensed, I enquired of Grimmett whether he was happy with the shape of the ball. His answer gave me little satisfaction. He implied that I must be finding something wrong with it judging by the number of full tosses I had been serving up. Referring the matter to Bill Woodfull I suggested that he ask the umpires to try putting the ball through the gauge, as I was quite sure it was completely off balance. They did that, and came out with a different ball. With my first delivery after the break Len Darling, fielding at short leg, caught Walters. Facing up to his first delivery Wyatt failed to contact one that collided with his middle stump. Walter Hammond, England's Bradman, came in on a hat-trick. He just managed to tickle the first ball with the inside edge of his bat and it streaked off between Oldfield's legs to the fence on the fine leg boundary. I bowled him with the fourth delivery of the over. England's score had slumped from 0 for 68 to 3 for 72 on a shirt-front wicket which had offered no hopeful prospects whatever for spin. Hendren and Leyland then took control for England, and they finally declared at 627 for 9 wickets. My contribution was 7 for 189 from 59 overs.

Several of our batsmen had contracted a throat infection during the game – Bradman and Chipperfield were the worst affected – but fortunately Stan McCabe came to the rescue with a splendid century, receiving great support from Bill Brown and Bill Woodfull. When my turn came to bat at number nine we still had to score 58 runs to save a follow on, which would have seen us batting under great difficulties with our team medically unfit. Here was a chance to atone for my match-losing performance at Lord's.

Batting with Chipperfield again, and then with fast bowler Tim Wall, we managed to hold the fort for the best part of two hours while we slowly accumulated those 58 runs, and 14 more besides. Immediately upon saving the follow on Woodfull sent twelfth man Ben Barnett out with drinks and a message telling us to carry on in exactly the same style for the remainder of the day – about four hours. The compliment was too much for us. Our chests and heads swelled at our captain's complimentary message. We went looking for runs with gay abandon. My partner soon fell foul of a magnificent return from the boundary which hit the stumps side-on to bring about his demise and the end of the innings.

In those days it took about six weeks for letters to travel to us from home. The next batch to arrive after that eventful match made us fully aware of the anxiety our tailend partnership had caused amongst our own folk who had been listening in loyally on the newfangled radio. In almost every letter an enquiry was made as to what sort of drink Woodfull had sent out to us when the follow on had been saved.

A few days after the game I received a cheque for one hundred pounds sterling from an Australian admirer named James Foley. Jim was a Tasmanian who served in World War I and never returned to his profession of mining engineering in northwestern Tasmania. Instead he went out to Nigeria where he became the owner of a prosperous tin mine. His cheque, which represented a very substantial part of the total amount paid to each of us for the whole tour by the Board of Control, started off a friendship with the Australian expatriate which lasted until Foley's death during World War II.

Throughout my sallies into English history as I trooped about the United Kingdom I often came face to face with historic vandalism committed in the name of patriotism by Oliver Cromwell and his cohorts. Never having developed any pronounced admiration for his particular brand of tyranny, I followed his devastations throughout England and Ireland right from the time I first saw Revolution House in Derbyshire, where the initial plans for that seventeenth century revolution were secretly laid.

Late in the 1934 tour my interest in Cromwell's behaviour stood me in good stead at Chequers, the beautiful Buckinghamshire home donated by Lord and Lady Leigh in the early 1920s as the perpetual residence of the reigning English Prime Minister.

There in that stately home my interest in history blossomed. Firstly I came to the rescue of Prime Minister Ramsay MacDonald in supplying the dates of the reign of King Stephen, when our host had some difficulty estimating the age of a magnificent oak tree at his back door. Grateful, I suppose, for my timely assistance, MacDonald, resplendent in his Savile Row suit and his profuse mop of blue-grey hair, gave me a personally conducted tour of the historic mementoes entrusted to Chequers. When we came to the Cromwell Room I noted that his Caledonian approach to the atmosphere contained therein resembled my own. There I read the very letter that Cromwell wrote home to his family to describe his great victory at Marston Moor; 'God made them as stubble to our swords' was, I thought, an incongruous remark for an Englishman to make about the sudden demise of so many of his own countrymen. Ramsay MacDonald, who is remembered these days mainly for his pacificism as leader of the English Labour Party in the days before World War II, seemed to share my view. He pointed out a hideous mask fixed high up on the wall. It had a massive forehead cover and in the middle of that forehead was a large protuberance designed to cover the unsightly carbuncle which disfigured the noble Oliver's appearance so drastically that his two daughters absolutely refused to have their father take part in any household hospitality unless he donned the mask which they had had specially made for him. No wonder, perhaps, that he acted in such an anti-social fashion.

Bristol has always been a popular cricket venue for Australian tourists. There is a hearty air about the western seaport which suggests to the visitor that it has developed proudly from the great days when it was the very heart of the sailing ship industry.

No man can walk the streets of that great port without coming in touch with three or four readily recognizable pieces of history.

Firstly, it took a terrible hiding from Hitler's Luftwaffe during the nightly raids early in World War II when Germany tried to put the port out of action.

Secondly, there are ever present signs which recall the marvellous stories of Bristol in the days of John Cabot, who sailed from there to America, and of Francis Drake, Martin Frobisher, Humphrey Gilbert and many others who played their parts on the high seas more or less as pirates under licence.

Thirdly, there is the old pub, the Landogger Trow, where you can lean comfortably on the bar and try to recall your childhood impressions of Robert Louis Stevenson's superlative story *Treasure Island.* The Landogger Trow is said to have provided the inspiration for the great Scotsman when he was weaving his tale of Long John Silver.

Bristol is busy. Every second establishment seemed to me to be devoted to the insurance business, which I realized was appropriate enough when one considered the great need for marine cover for cargo leaving the docks. But by far the most fertile imagination fodder that Bristol provided for me were the four flat-topped steel stanchions, about three feet in diameter and four feet high, situated in the Corn Exchange. They are affectionately known as 'The Nails' by the broad-vowelled citizens who hurry about the marketplace in the centre of the city. On enquiry I discovered that they had been called 'The Nails' since the time of those semi-buccaneering men of the sea whom I have already mentioned. Returning from a profitable sally on the Spanish Main, as a certain area of the mid-Atlantic was known to them, men like Hawkins, Frobisher and Co would bring their ill-gotten gains into the marketplace to sell by public auction. On knocking a sale down to the highest bidder, the salesman would insist that the purchase price agreed upon be placed on 'The Nail' beside the auctioneer. That was elementary enough, but what tickled my fancy about the whole transaction is that this was where our time-worn phrase, 'cash on the nail', originated.

Such gems of history turn up frequently to exalt the traveller who keeps his ears and eyes wide open.

Sir James Barrie, who gave us Peter Pan, was my host in his flat at the Adelphi Terrace overlooking Pall Mall. Arthur Mailey, who came on the tour as a pressman, was responsible for the invitation, which was received with open arms. My association with Barrie had given me great pleasure over a number of years, although the great Scotsman would not have been aware of it.

Along with Hans Ebeling, Alan Kippax, Stan McCabe, A.P. Lucas and Mailey himself we landed ourselves in Barrie's sitting room straight from Lord's Cricket Ground where we had been busily engaged in a match with the Gentlemen of England, a fixture which has since departed from the list of Australian matches. Barrie was waiting for us: a tiny man dressed in a dark three-piece suit which displayed a heavily linked gold watch chain anchored in his vest pocket. His ample black moustache drooped rather untidily over a mouth which held a large shiny pipe from which a vast cloud of smoke was being powerfully emitted.

He made us welcome in the softest voice imaginable – it reminded me immediately of Maurice Tate and Neville Cardus, both of whom were extremely quietly spoken – and after doing justice to our host's table we settled back for the after-dinner discussion for which Barrie had long been famous.

He was mad about cricket, a fact which came as a surprise to me, who had imagined that cricket had remained a secret to the Caledonians. He had come south in pursuit of his literary career, he told us, had settled in Kent, and in due course had got together his own team to play socially.

'Slow bowling,' he said, 'was my forté. I am perhaps the slowest bowler the game has seen.'

He went on to describe his pace as so slow that he could rush forward to retrieve the ball in mid-air if he discovered that he had made some fundamental mistake in its launching.

Noticing my air of incredulity he proceeded to give me an example of his style. Bowling one day on his home ground in Kent he launched his customary leg break, and on examining it critically exclaimed, 'My God he's out.'

He sat down at the crease, he said, to watch as the delivery made its way up the wicket, evaded the bat, and leant up against the off stump, gently removing just one bail.

The number of times that I have watched that Barrie leg break leaning up against the off stump and recalled with admiration the spell-binding personality of that tiny tale-spinner is beyond my calculation. I still do it.

At Canterbury in 1934 Arthur Mailey invited me to join him in a Saturday night dinner party for four which he reckoned I would find interesting.

I jumped at the chance. Mailey was an unusual character. He had a reputation for whimsical humour, and he was one of those likeable people who made sure he invariably got the laugh against himself. I joined him in his private dining room to find that Tom Clarke, a Fleet Street journalist who later occupied a university Chair of Journalism, was already present and in animated discussion with Will Dyson, a member of the celebrated artistic Australian family of which Ned, the author of such Australian classics as *Fact'ry 'Ands* and *The Golden Shanty,* was the leading light.

Dinner began. The conversation and the wine were excellent. Cricket, to my delight, was rarely touched upon. At that very time the King, George V, was suffering an indisposition which had caused the Fleet Street fraternity no little concern. This of course came up for comment and led to a memorable dissection of the manner in which great newspapers sought to offer their news in the most enticing form to catch the public's eye and thereby sell newspapers in profit-making volume.

Tom Clarke, then working on one of the great London morning dailies, was asked what his paper, then appearing in tabloid form and one of the very first to do so, would do with the front page were the King to succumb to his illness that very night.

'Right across the page in banner headlines with a photo and nothing else in sight,' was his immediate response.

To me who knew nothing whatever about the mysteries of presenting a newspaper to its customers, it seemed that Clarke's opinion was absolutely final, because it was the very first opinion that had so far been accepted without rather prolonged discussion. With that resolved Dyson asked what would be done if Edward,

Prince of Wales, were to depart this world. Clarke said that he would most certainly be given the whole front page too, if there happened to be no other piece of Empire-shattering news to claim part of that important area.

Arthur Mailey then wanted to know how the editors would react if both the Prince of Wales and Don Bradman were to make their exits simultaneously. That query from the puckish Australian furrowed the brows of the pundits ranged around the festive board. Talk went on at great length about the relative importance of the news items from so many different angles that I felt I needed Bartholomew's Atlas to help in deciding the many scattered areas of the British Empire which would be deeply concerned with the two items.

It was eventually decided that both would be displayed on the front page. The Prince of Wales would occupy the top left-hand side of the front page, Bradman the top right.

Such was the popularity of Don Bradman in England in 1934.

Early in the 1934 tour we received an invitation to visit Windsor Castle.

As we waited for the call to board our bus I took quite a ribbing from my team-mates for wearing dark brown shoes with my dark grey suit. It was not done, they said, in the best of circles. Their point was taken and we set out for the Castle. En route Hans Ebeling gave us a stirring rendition of 'Old Father Thames Rolls Down to the Mighty Sea' in his deepest baritone, followed by 'Silent Night' as an encore. It was never easy to coax Hans to burst into song, but it was hard to stop him on that lovely Sunday afternoon. Perhaps the thought of meeting a King descended from the House of Hanover warmed Ebeling's Scandinavian blood. Whenever the subject of my Hibernian lineage came up in conversation – which was often – Hans would say, 'We Saxons must always stick together.'

The gates opened on our arrival and we drove in over the moat and past the keep to be met with due pomp by Lord Willingdon, a recent Viceroy of India, and the King's Secretary Lord Wigram. Having been ushered into the presence of Queen Mary we walked out into one of the big squares covered with a magnificent lawn and waited in the sunshine for the King to join us.

In accordance with the requests of my team-mates, who were still ragging me about my rugged taste in shoes, I stood well hidden in the back row. His Majesty made his entrance wearing a grey panama hat, a navy blue serge suit with the trousers sporting their creases down the sides – appropriately, I thought, after all he was known as 'the Sailor King' – and more importantly, you've probably guessed it, he wore tan shoes. It was not for me to take a back seat any longer. My taste was in line with royalty. I had taken a step up on the social ladder and I wasted no time in letting them all know – sotto voce.

We had our afternoon tea on that enormous lawn with their Majesties, then the Queen said, 'I think, George, we should stand here for the boys to take their photographs.'

I wondered to myself just how many people there were amongst the fifty million English who had the right to address HM as 'George'. Queen Mary impressed me as the stateliest person I had ever seen. Dressed in a bone-coloured gown which reached almost to the ground, her tiny waistline suggested that some undergarments were doing a mighty important job amidships. She wore a tiny hat and leaned elegantly on a bone-coloured parasol that set her off just right. She was a most imposing woman. I couldn't help trying to visualize the dilemma I would have found myself in trying to explain where I had been if I came home at 2 o'clock in the morning.

After tea we were taken for an inspection of the Castle garden, where we listened to the band playing to the crowd who were flocking to the Windsor Park outside the grounds, and then on a conducted tour of the Castle itself.

One or two historical relics, souvenirs if you like, took the eye of schoolteacher O'Reilly. There was the steel suit of armour that belonged, they said, to Henry VIII. Why he wanted it I could not work out, I never heard of him riding valiantly into the fray, and it would have needed the biggest draught horse ever bred in Britain to have carried Henry in that suit. Two men like me could have stepped inside it.

The next piece of history that caught my imagination was the ring which Elizabeth I wore on her right hand.

Those lucky people who are conversant with English history will remember that the 'Virgin Queen', Elizabeth I, left no direct descendant to the throne. She had gone out of her way, as a matter of fact, to make sure that there was no clear-cut claimant for her job. She had arranged the execution of two of her relatives, Lady Jane Grey and Mary Queen of Scots, both of whom lost their lives on the chopping block. But Mary Queen of Scots had played a dirty trick on her: she bore a son, James Stuart, who was lowered as a baby from a window in a little room I saw in Edinburgh Castle, where helping hands a few hundred feet below took him off to safety.

This son of Mary and Lord Darnley had become James VI of Scotland by the time Elizabeth's reign was drawing to a close, and he was duly named as the successor to the English throne. But there was no way in the wide world that James would have dared to visit England if Elizabeth were living. He knew what had happened to his mother. So when the English ambassadors made their way to Edinburgh in 1603 to tell James that Elizabeth had departed this earth and that James himself was rightful King, they had to produce that great diamond, which rests now in Windsor Castle, before James Stuart would budge an inch towards London. He knew Elizabeth would not have budged without the ring safely on her finger. Neither would I, if it were mine.

I was not told where the enormous diamond had come from, and was so busy pondering its value that I forgot to ask. It certainly did not come from Kimberley or anywhere along the Orange or Vaal Rivers in South Africa. Those sources had not been tapped in Elizabeth's time. I guess therefore it must have come from India. Whatever country produced it, I bet they were loath to let it go.

To cap the afternoon's history lesson I was able to inspect the musket ball which accounted for the life of one of England's greatest heroes, Horatio Lord Nelson, who unluckily happened to impede its progress at the battle of Trafalgar. I had recently had the chance to visit Nelson's old flagship, HMS *Victory*, and I had seen the spot where the great admiral fell. Here then was the chance to pay final respects to a man whom I had greatly admired from the moment I first made his acquaintance, at the age of eight or nine, in a childish history book. I could see the French ships lined up in battle formation so close that snipers using blunderbusses whilst perching in the rigging were able to take pot-shots at sailors on the deck. There was the gallant Captain Hardy, who rushed to his leader's side when he fell, and the lanky Doctor Sawkins who tended Nelson in the surgery which Sawkins must have had to kneel to enter. It was not until I saw Nelson's effigy in Westminster Abbey that I realized he was such a tiny man. It is a remarkable coincidence that the two great wartime leaders produced by France and England, Napoleon and Nelson, were so incredibly small that they could easily have ridden in the Melbourne Cup.

I had the opportunity to go further with the Nelson connection when later on we played a County match against Kent at Canterbury. We stayed at the Royal Fountain Hotel there, and the presence of many portraits of Lord Nelson encouraged me to discover that this little pub was the one chosen by the admiral as his trysting place with Lady Emma Hamilton, who was Nelson's partner in one of the most charming love stories of that war-torn time. The Royal Fountain charms no more. Adolf Hitler's Luftwaffe blew it to pieces during World War II.

His Majesty King George V proved to be an interested and gracious host. He certainly gave us the impression that he was keenly interested in cricket, and especially in the Test series which had just begun. He mentioned nothing about bodyline. I found myself wondering, as the afternoon's proceedings drew to a close, whether he would secretly have liked to take one or two of us aside to get some first-hand information on what had really happened in his far-flung South Seas dominion during the summer of 1932-33. Having a fair idea of human nature I came to the personal conclusion that he would have loved to, but of course he didn't. Couldn't, I suppose.

We renewed acquaintance with him when he paid his accustomed visit to the Lord's Test, and in the few passing words he had with us as he went down the line he made it quite plain that he had enjoyed our previous meeting.

6 May 1933, the bridal party. *From left*: Stan Jones, Lucy Jones (nee Herbert), Bill O'Reilly, Molly O'Reilly (nee Herbert), Jack Fingleton, Kathleen Lees

Peter and Patricia O'Reilly in the early 1940s

With Sydney Grammar under 14s in 1937

With Stan McCabe at Sydney Central Station after coming back from South Africa in 1936

The 1935-36 Australians as baseballers in a Testimonial benefit game in Johannesburg for former South African captain Jock Cameron's widow. *From left:* Rowe, Richardson, McCabe, O'Reilly, McCormick, Fingleton, Brown, O'Brien, Barnett, Darling, Grimmett, Oldfield

The Richardson-Grimmett Testimonial match, Adelaide Oval, November 1937. *Back row:* Vic Jackson, Charlie Walker, Bill Brown, Ginty Lush, Keith Rigg, Chuck Fleetwood-Smith, Frank Ward, Lindsay Hassett. *Middle:* J.D. Scott, Ross Gregory, Jack Fingleton, Ernie McCormick, Bill O'Reilly, Morris Sievers, Bob Hynes, Ray Robinson, A.G. Jenkins. *Front:* Jackie Badcock, Bert Oldfield, Vic Richardson, Don Bradman, Clarrie Grimmett, Stan McCabe, Arthur Chipperfield

The 1938 Australians and their hosts at the Belfast Cricket Club, Northern Ireland

The Australians in New Zealand, 1946. *Standing:* W. Watts (scorer), D. Tallon, K.R. Miller, W.J. O'Reilly, E.R.H. Toshack, B. Dooland, R.A. Hamence, E.C. Yeomans (manager). *Seated:* I.W. Johnson, C.V. McCool, A.L. Hassett, W.A. Brown (captain), S.G. Barnes, K.D. Meuleman, R.R. Lindwall. Note the logos on the blazers

The gentlemen of the press take the field on the rest day during the first Test against the Englishmen in 1946. *From left:* Arthur Mailey, Vivian Jenkins (UK), Vic Richardson, Percy Beames, Bill O'Reilly, George Duckworth (UK), Jack Fingleton, Bill Bowes (UK), Brian Sellers (UK)

With Clarrie Grimmett in Brisbane during the first Test of the 1946-47 series against England

Chegwyn's team at Mackay, Queensland, Easter 1949. *From left:* Bill Beath, Arthur Morris, Bill Donaldson, Walter South, Jack Chegwyn, Bill O'Reilly, Ernie Laidler, Charlie O'Brien, Ron Kissell, Alan Walker, Ray Lindwall

With the Duke of Beaufort and the Duke of Edinburgh at the opening of the Lord's Museum in 1953

Brisbane, 1960. With (*from left*) golfers Bill Brown, Lindsay Hassett, Ray Lindwall and Jack Fingleton

On the way to the middle to bowl the first ball to Don Bradman at the opening of the Sir Donald Bradman Memorial Oval at Bowral in September 1976

To round off my story of George V in 1934 I must add that he was quick to show his sympathy for our team-mate Don Bradman, when that young man, hospitalized at the close of the 1934 tour, was recovering from an emergency appendectomy. After our return from our invasion of Scotland, where we had laid the Highlands low at Forres way up on Moray Firth, our vice-captain was taken off to the Park Lane Private Hospital, run by the Australian surgeon Sir Douglas Shields. The operation took over four hours.

Bradman's condition became a matter of national importance. The little private hospital in Park Lane was avalanched with phone calls from concerned cricket lovers. With the idea perhaps of trying to cope with this problem the hospital officials thought fit to read out the bulletin with which Shields had presented them after his regular morning visit. On the morning after the operation the bulletin for the day was, 'Bradman's condition is serious. His temperature is still rising'. That bulletin continued to be read out throughout the day. You can imagine what effect that little word 'still' would have had during the late afternoon.

A friend of mine, a member of the Baltic Exchange over in the City, rang me during the afternoon to say that he had just read of Bradman's death on the ticker tape in their busy salesroom. Apparently someone, conscious of the fact that a scoop was in the offing, decided to pre-empt the event which Dr Shields' thermometer seemed to be prophesying. During that hectic afternoon only three Australians – McCabe, Darling and O'Reilly – were at our London headquarters, the Langham Hotel. We were in a state of siege, with messenger boys chasing us throughout the building to answer phone enquiries, one of which came from Buckingham Palace. It was made by Lord Wigram, the King's Secretary, and I was the man whose turn it was to take the call. The King was deeply concerned about Bradman's condition and wanted to know if his team-mates could give him the latest news. All I could do was to inform Lord Wilgram that we, too, had been provided with the same disturbing bulletin as everybody else. Of course we all know now that Don Bradman, although he was certainly very sick at the time, subsequently became one of the very few people privileged to read his own obituary.

That was the full extent of my dealings with royalty. When we went back to England in 1938 much had happened in the House of Windsor. King George V had died, King Edward VIII had abdicated, and King George VI had been enthroned. When the time came for the accustomed visit to Windsor Castle, the Royal Court was in mourning as a mark of respect for one of their family, and it was closed to all official visitors.

19 Early Retirement

The opportunity to tour represented the greatest windfall of my young life. The cherished friendships engendered amongst my team-mates and others filled me with joy, and the chances given me to meet interesting people and to come face to face with places about which I had read with avid interest was like a dream come true.

Sailing away from England on the way home, I felt I was a much better Australian than before I had set out, but at the same time I was certain that I had not seen a better country than my own and that I owed an enormous debt, unpayable, to my grandfather Peter O'Reilly, who had folded up his Irish tent and headed into the southern seas sixty-nine years before.

Perhaps 'unpayable' is not quite correct. Two days after my return to Sydney my wife Molly gave birth to a beautiful blonde headed daughter, Patricia Mary. I fully realized that Molly had been literally carrying the baby for me, and I had some hard work and hard thinking to do back in Australia.

I went back to my job at Kogarah High School, where it immediately became clear to me that a tremendous decision stared me in the face. The terms of my employment as a permanent teacher with the Education Department were such that I receded beyond the horizon in terms of advancement with every spell of unpaid leave applied for and granted. For every day I had off from school to play cricket I automatically fell behind all those people with whom I had started my teaching career back in 1926. The problem was clear as day. If I continued to play cricket I would fall so far behind my contemporaries in seniority that it would be stupid to carry on with the job of teaching.

I liked teaching, and although the life of a touring Australian cricketer also held its charms for me, I decided to retire from cricket at the beginning of the 1934-35 season.

A couple of sympathetic efforts were made in an attempt to help me decide to continue my playing career. David Jones Ltd, with whom I had started my metropolitan cricket activities in the Moore Park Competition, offered to employ me in the Sports Department, offering me full support in regard to time off for cricket. As a counter to that Bertram Stevens, the New South Wales Premier, offered to arrange an appointment to the staff of Sydney Boys' High School on condition that I went back to evening lectures to complete an Arts Course to which cricket had applied the closure in 1932. My inclination was to continue my teaching career, but even though the Department was prepared to make me such an offer, I realized that it did not really resolve the problem I was facing.

Then Sydney Grammar School came to my assistance with an offer of employment which satisfied me completely. I was asked to attend the surgery of an eminent eye surgeon who was also the Chairman of Trustees of Sydney Grammar. He told me that the school was prepared to make me a member of their staff on the strength of a reference they had obtained from a source within the Department as to my ability in the classroom, but he said that he could not give me any assurance at that stage as to what arrangements could be made to allow me to continue playing cricket. That left me up in the air for the moment, but the headmaster put my mind at rest in the first minute of our conversation, when I went to his office at the school the same afternoon.

In the course of that interview I was assured that I would be a very welcome member of the staff, that I 'must', not 'could', carry on with my cricket career, and that I would be granted leave on half pay for every day I was on cricket leave. I accepted the job there and then.

During the two weeks it took for me to quit the Education Department I must admit that I spent many a troubled moment worrying whether I had done the right thing. There were those amongst my friends who thought I was taking a giant step into the darkness by quitting a job which offered permanent employment and an assured superannuation pension upon retirement. But in deciding to join Grammar I made the best decision of my working life. That decision, which caused me so much soul-searching, conditioned me for the many decisions that were ahead for me. It taught me to make up my mind quickly, to think clearly, and to reject all the backing and filling which takes most of the fun out of life.

I spent five very happy years at Grammar, aware that in Bert Dettmann I had a completely sympathetic boss who handled me on such friendly terms that he won my complete trust and admiration. The favourable conditions of employment gave my family much more security, and we have always held Grammar high in our affection and been loud in its praise since our association with it.

As a result of my 'retirement' I played only a couple of first-class games in the 1934-35 season: one was the Woodfull-Ponsford Testimonial match, the other a Sheffield Shield game against Victoria. But the following summer, after my move to Sydney Grammar, I was back in full harness and available, and selected for, the tour of South Africa in 1935-36.

20 South Africa

Our Australian tour of South Africa in the 1935-36 season was by far the most pleasant experience of my cricket career. The South African approach to cricket appealed to me immensely, indeed their attitude to the game reminded me of the jovial sporting feeling that pervaded the memorable matches I enjoyed during my sojourn as a teacher in Western New South Wales.

The composition of our side could not have been improved upon socially. Every member was prepared to carry his full weight and responsibility in the crowded list of social engagements that highlighted the tour. Every one of us made a host of friends.

Our skipper, Victor York Richardson—'Yorker' as we called him—although he was 41 years of age and past his cricket best, performed magnificantly in an 'off the field' display which in my experience has never been surpassed by an Australian cricket captain. The South African cricket officials, aware of his forthright honesty and his infectious good humour, accepted him with such obvious gratitude that the greatest difficulty we encountered was in coping with their overwhelming hospitality.

We took fourteen men on tour. Don Bradman had declared himself unavailable as he was immersed in moving his business interests from Sydney to Adelaide, where he had decided to start a career in the sharebroking industry under the aegis of Harry Hodgetts, a member of the Australian Board of Control.

Everybody in the team knew that this was sure to be Yorker's swan song as a captain, a job which he had been carrying out in South Australia with great credit for a period longer than most of his team-mates could remember. With Bradman about to appear on the South Australian cricket scene, we guessed that the leadership for the tour was being handed to Richardson as an 'ex gratia' gesture for good and faithful service. To a man, we resolved that he should enjoy it to the full. The politics surrounding the arrangement never surfaced once on tour. Victor led the team with his accustomed flair, unruffled by the fact that his aggregate of Test runs amounted to 84 at an average of 16. The question of him dropping himself from the Test arena never entered our heads.

The South Africans at that period were experiencing embarrassing difficulties in maintaining the great reputation they had been steadily building in international cricket. The death of Neville Quinn, their gifted fast-medium left-arm bowler, had dealt them an awful blow. On tour in Australia as a member of HB (Jock) Cameron's 1931-32 Springbok side, Quinn's ability was obvious. He had Bradman dropped twice early in the first Test, and had him caught behind for 2 in the second Test. He was a similar type of bowler to Bill Johnston, the talented Victorian left-hander, and when I first saw Johnston in the 1945-46 season the likeness impressed me sufficiently to forecast a great future for him.

To make matters even worse for our hosts their great wicket-keeper-batsman-captain Jock Cameron had died of a fever aboard ship on the way home from England, where he had played with great distinction on their 1935 tour, when the South Africans had won the only completed Test.

Our manager on the tour was the genial Harold Rowe, a capable left-handed batsman who had played first-class cricket for Western Australia before representing that State on the Board of Control. He was a valued friend and trusty companion to each one of us, and at the tour's end we classed him as the most likeable character ever to travel along with us as manager.

At the opening press conference in Durban, after we had alighted from the good ship *Ulysses* of the Blue Funnel Line and had been rushed off to the Royal Hotel to take block for our first encounter with South African hospitality, Harold made the most rewarding faux pas of his happy life. To introduce a little humour in his reply to the toast of welcome, he told the story of the timid bowler confronted with the giant form of Warwick Armstrong, the Australian captain of the early 1920s. Armstrong's enormous pads and heavily-taxed trousers completely obscured the stumps. The bat looked like a plaything. One look was enough for the nervous bowler, who turned to the umpire and said, 'What do I do, ump? I can't see a sign of the stumps.'

'Just bowl,' said the umpire. Scratching his head, the bowler asked, 'What will you do if I appeal for leg-before-wicket?'

'Leave it to me – if you hit him in the pads he's out, but if you hit him in the arse it's a wide,' was the simple answer.

It went over well, as it has done for the past sixty years, but Rowe was unaware that the welcome was being broadcast throughout the length and breadth of the Union of South Africa, and also in the dominions of Southern and Northern Rhodesia for good measure. He had no cause to regret his indiscretion. Everywhere he went he was congratulated for his enterprising repartee, much to his embarrassment when the ladies joined in to express their admiration.

It was on that happy tour that an Australian touring team made its very first trip by air, albeit unofficially. Having heard stirring accounts of the grandeur of the Kruger National Park north of Johannesburg, where the legendary African wildlife could be observed at close quarters, we put the hard word on Harold Rowe to arrange a Sunday return flight to the reserve for the whole touring party. Even though we had all solemnly signed the contract which bound us to the rule that we should not commit ourselves to the dangers of air travel – the Board obviously had some fears about compensation payments – Harold arranged for a plane to be at our disposal. It was a German Junkers. I am not aware of anyone else having misgivings about our safety, after all it was seven years since Charles Kingsford Smith had safely flown the Pacific so it would have been quite undignified for an Australian to have jibbed at the flight, but I must admit that I had some personal misgivings when, on approaching our destination, complete cloud cover made it impossible for the pilot to observe any obstacles which might impede our progress. We soon realized that he was as lost as we were. Radar was still a long way off in those days.

With 44 wickets in his South African Test bag Clarrie Grimmett made cricket history at the same time as he gave our hosts, by example, a valuable lesson in the art of leg spin bowling. His claim to be acknowledged as the best slow bowler ever will certainly still be recognized by South African enthusiasts who had the good luck to see him in action in their country.

We were given a good look at the blossoming talents of the South African batting genius Dudley Nourse, who was just setting out on his remarkable career. In the second Test, played on the beautiful Wanderers ground in Johannesburg, Nourse displayed his unflappable personality when we held him for twenty minutes on a 'pair'. He then proceeded to tear off the 231 runs which made that innings the best South African performance of the tour.

We were left with 399 to get in the fourth innings of that Test, and on a wearing pitch it looked likely that the Springboks would square the series. Fortunately for us it was then that Stan McCabe produced the second of the three sublime Test innings which are recalled every time Stan's name is mentioned. Brown was out early, but McCabe scored his first 50 in 40 minutes and we were 1 for 85 at stumps on the third day. On the fourth day Fingleton played a sensible defensive role while McCabe did just as he liked with the bowling. Australia was 2 wickets for 274 when, with an approaching storm darkening the ground, the Springbok captain Herbert Wade appealed against the light from the field: he was afraid that one of his men might be injured by a thunderbolt from Stan McCabe's bat.

The rest of that game was washed out, but we won the third, fourth and fifth Tests to give us the series four Tests to nil.

Several prolific opening partnerships from Jack Fingleton and Bill Brown highlighted Australia's overwhelming superiority in the Tests. For Fingleton it was just the opportunity he needed to restore the confidence which deserted him when his omission from the 1934 tour of England turned his burgeoning career sour.

Grimmett's 44 wickets at 14.59 owed much to Richardson's fearless fielding at short leg, where he took five catches in the final South African innings of the series. Both those performances are still high on the list of record-breaking feats. My own contribution was 27 wickets at 17.59, satisfying enough even if it was 17 wickets less than my friendly rival.

My interest in South African cricket, sharpened by my profound respect for the wonderful spirit with which all their players entered the fray, was adequately rewarded when I had the pleasure of seeing Barry Richards in action for South Australia early in the 1970s. Richards played some of the finest innings I have seen, and it was fortunate for Greg Chappell that he was given the opportunity to use Richards as a near-perfect example so early in his career.

It was a matter of great regret to me that Barry Richards was unable, through no fault of his own, to enjoy a full term in international cricket. His complete command of intelligent use of his feet would have been a precious lesson to succeeding groups of deprived young Australian batsmen. Footwork, to my sorrow, in an age of over-emphasized speed bowling, has disappeared from view.

21 On Captaincy

No sooner, so it seemed, had we returned from South Africa, than we had to face up to the Englishmen again, this time under the captaincy of fast bowler Gubby Allen in the summer of 1936-37. Allen had been one of Douglas Jardine's pace battery during the bodyline summer, but he had been a conscientious objector so far as the war on the field was concerned, sticking to perfectly orthodox tactics, and he was one of the few members of Jardine's side with whom we had been able to maintain reasonably cordial relations.

Australia was led for the first time by Don Bradman.

In the newspaper column which it is still my privilege to contribute to the *Sydney Morning Herald,* I have laid claims for many years now that my collie dog shows all the requirements for making a reasonable success of the responsibilities of leading an Australain cricket team. At this late stage of his career I reluctantly admit that I have never owned such a dog, nor am I ever likely to acquire one.

When I was just a boy in the bush I was the proud owner of a dog about twice my size, a 'kangaroo dog' named Nip. Fond memories I have of him too – no rabbit's life was worth living once Nip had laid eyes on him. But as a country boy I refuse to condemn any self-respecting dog to the misery of a dog's life in the confines of the city.

So far as I am concerned the only worthwhile association between dogs and cricket is in Thomas E. Spencer's poem, 'How MacDougal Topped the Score', wherein the men of Molongo challenge the men of Piper's Flat to a game of cricket, the losing side to pay for lunch. Molongo made only 66, but Piper's Flat's chances of receiving a free feed did not look promising with 9 wickets down for 17. Enter MacDougal. A Scotsman by birth, MacDougal had not actually taken part in a game of cricket before, but he was partial to a free lunch and had done some secret training in the company of his sheepdog, Pincher. MacDougal spooned the first ball he received back towards the bowler, shouted 'Fetch', and Pincher did the rest. Molongo 66, Piper's Flat 9-67 (MacDougal 50 not out). In my mind's eye, Pincher has always been a collie.

Which brings me, in a roundabout way, back to the subject of captaincy.

Was Bradman a great captain? Of course he was. His winning record establishes that fact beyond argument.

But let us consider the facts that made him a winning captain. Did his own personal batting contributions add inordinately to his reputation? Of course they did. Do any members of his team remember brilliant manoeuvres or decisions from him that swayed the outcome of a game? I doubt it. As a team-mate I regarded Bradman as a tremendous team bonus. To have him on my side meant two things. Firstly, I would not be facing the job of bowling at him. Secondly, he usually scored enough runs to make my bowling job easy.

I never knew him to show great enterprise in schemeful thinking, and for that I was grateful. I would detest playing with a leader who made me think he was big-noting himself. The same goes for every person who skippered a side of which I was a member.

Of course I always took it for granted that a bowler was highly unlikely ever to be asked to lead. His responsibilities, so it was generally inferred, were too demanding, too physical for his brain to be expected to be functioning efficiently at all relevant times. That he was a nitwit was proven beyond doubt by the fact that he had decided to become a bowler in the first place. This subject is always governed by the premise that the bowler is cricket's labourer.

His job is to boil the billy and run the messages. No wonder I have had constant recourse to my collie dog.

I invite you to take a look at the story of Australian cricket captaincy over the past sixty-five years.

It began with 'The Big Ship', Warwick Armstrong, the enormous Victorian who played Test cricket at 22 stone (140 kgs) and skippered Australia immediately after World War I, setting up a reputation for invincibility. The museum at the Melbourne Cricket Ground supplies excellent proof of Armstrong's tremendous displacement by preserving one of his cream cricket shirts. It is so big that it seems it could easily be used as a tent to house the luncheon arrangements.

Despite his bulk, he was a very talented cricketer. A punishing batsman who had only to lean on a ball to make it go back past the bowler at hand-warming speed, he bowled his slowish leg breaks sufficiently well to become one of the few bowlers to scrape together 100 English Test scalps. In other words he was one of Australia's greatest all-rounders.

Strangely enough, you never hear much about him. Why?

Because he was horribly unpopular with cricket's hierarchy. He was the sole survivor of those six great players who had thumbed their noses at the Australian Board of Cricket Control in 1912 and had wrecked the tour of England that season by refusing to join it. His five mates were all out of the game by 1920, when Test cricket was resumed after the 1914-18 war. Two of them, Victor Trumper and Tibby Cotter, were dead. Trumper had succumbed to an incurable kidney complaint in 1915. Tibby Cotter lost his life as a member of the Australian Light Horse during the war.

Armstrong had to cop the flak that still surrounded him for his part as a member of the 'Big Six' as they were called. How he was approved for the captaincy the Lord alone knows. Then, as now, the Board members appointed the captain from the list of players handed them by the selectors. Rumour has it that Armstrong sneaked through the vote with a majority of one, but he made his claim as the best captain ever, despite his powerful executive detractors, because he led an extraordinarily strong team.

More importantly, he led a team which possessed outstanding bowling talent.

With two fast bowlers, Jack Gregory and the Tasmanian Ted McDonald, and spinners Arthur Mailey and Armstrong himself, Australia had enormous strike power and proved far too good for the English batsmen. McDonald, after touring with Armstrong's 1921 side in England, spent the remainder of his career as an outstanding member of the Lancashire County Club.

Armstrong couldn't help being dubbed a great captain. He never lost a Test. Australia won all five Tests in Australia in 1920-21 and the first three in England in 1921, the final two being drawn.

Let's look at what happened in the following sixty years. Herbie Collins led the team with diminishing success after 'The Big Ship' retired, and it fell to the unhappy lot of Jack Ryder as captain to see that great side reduce itself to an array of extinct volcanoes – aided and abetted of course by a young English captain named Percy Chapman who ran away home with the Ashes in 1928-29. Ryder then lost the job to Bill Woodfull who took a team of kids to England in 1930 and regained the Ashes, mainly of course through the prodigious batting efforts of the youthful Don Bradman. However it should never be forgotten that Clarrie Grimmett's bowling efforts were also almost superhuman on that tour. With no real bowling support, he bowled 350 overs in the Tests and took 29 wickets against an English team which included Hobbs, Sutcliffe, Hammond, Duleepsinhji and Hendren.

Woodfull's reputation stands high amongst Australian captains. There is none of my time whom I would place ahead of him, but it was as well that he decided to make a final tour of England after the bodyline series. Had Woodfull not made that 1934 tour and regained the Ashes lost in 1933, cricket history would have treated him harshly. As it is, he is the only Australian captain to twice regain the Ashes in England.

Why? Because he had Bradman, and he also had the bowlers upon whom he could place full responsibility to do the job he wanted done. In his 1930 tour he had Grimmett, and in 1934 he had Grimmett and me. Together we took 53 of the 70 odd English Test wickets that fell.

Perhaps you have noticed that I am slowly but surely making the point that bowlers win cricket matches. Batsmen – some of them – fill cricket grounds; bowlers fill the opposition dressing rooms with unsuccessful batsmen. Ryder lost his captaincy because his bowling brigade was worn out. Jardine won the bodyline series because he had Larwood and Voce. Like Armstrong, Woodfull regained his great name when he had a real bowling combination – Grimmett and O'Reilly. The same combination took 71 wickets in the Tests against South Africa in 1935-36.

Then Bradman took over in 1936-37. We lost the first two Tests convincingly. England swamped us on wet wickets in Brisbane and Sydney, and Gubby Allen almost got away with the Ashes. Despite the inexcusable absence of Grimmett, some great innings from Bradman, McCabe, Fingleton and Badcock, and the bowling combination of Fleetwood-Smith (19 wickets) and O'Reilly (25 wickets), enabled us to hold onto the Ashes 3-2.

Bradman took the 1938 team to England and retained the Ashes, but only just. That series was squared, and it probably would have served the gifted Australian right if he had not been given the opportunity to redeem a somewhat tarnished leadership reputation by captaining that magnificent 1948 Australian team on tour in England. As a selector, Bradman had to bear his own portion of the responsibility for omitting Grimmett from the 1938 tour, and it was quite fitting that he should pay the penalty for it by only succeeding in squaring that series. Grimmett was still the world's best leg spinner. He was so much better than the man chosen to replace him on tour, Frank Ward, that I thought Ward was done an injury in being asked to try to do the job. Ward only played in one Test, the first, and it is simply unthinkable to me that in that final Test at the Oval, which England won by an innings and 579 runs, they could have made 903 runs – Hutton 364 – if I had had Grimmett to support me at the other end.

Bradman's reputation as a highly successful Australian captain was made on the 1948 tour to England. His bowlers, Lindwall, Miller and Bill Johnston saw to that, and of course one must not forget the priceless assistance given them by the English cricket legislators who had decreed that a new ball should be handed to them – the finest new ball trio Australia has ever produced – at the end of every 55th over. That was a belated attempt to destroy the dominance of the Australian leg spinners, and the results it produced served them right.

Bradman's sucessor was Lindsay Hassett, a consummate batsman with a second-to-none knowledge of the game, allied with a puckish personality that endeared him to all who knew him. Hassett won against South Africa in 1949-50, against England in 1950-51 and against the West Indies in 1951-52, then squared a home series against the Springboks before losing the Ashes to England in 1953.

It was left to Ian Johnson to preside over the dying throes of a once great team, as Herbie Collins had done before him. He lost consecutive Ashes series, in Australia in 1954-55 when Tyson and Statham tore the heart out of the Australian batting, and in England in 1956 when Jim Laker and Tony Lock – yet another great bowling combination, in case you hadn't noticed – proved our undoing.

And so, via Ian Craig, to Richie Benaud. Johnson had stayed long enought to welcome Benaud and Alan Davidson into the Australian team, but neither had proved to be quick developers. Australia's main bowling responsibilities in 1956 all rested on the shoulders of Lindwall and Miller, both of whom were well past their best.

Benaud was third cab on the rank when Ian Johnson's captaincy spot had to be filled after the chaotic 1956 tour of England. Johnson is a valued friend of mine. I know him to have been a highly knowledgeable cricketer, thoughtful, intelligent and kind. I referred to his tour as chaotic because he led a team which never looked to have the slightest chance of beating England. That team's vital players were completely over the hill. Benaud was not likely ever to be considered to fill Johnson's place – that fact was public property in 1956. Number one for the job was Queenslander Ron Archer, who suffered a knee injury of such severity that his cricket career, although he was three years younger than Benaud, was brought to an unfortunately early close. Second in line was Ian Craig, who held the job briefly but lost it through ill health. Those two can regard themselves as unlucky that illness and injury cost them the mantle of greatness which was providentially cast over Richie Benaud's broad shoulders when the gifted all-rounder was gathered in as a replacement.

Benaud's great reputation came to him as a fluke, but there was no fluke about his maintaining it. He was a very good bowler himself, and to support him he had great performers like Davidson and McKenzie. He led an up-and-coming side with just the right flavouring of young and vigorous bowlers that were necessary to put him in the box seat. Without gifted bowlers, supported by the usual quota of reliable, courageous batsmen, a leader is hardly worth a moment's examination when it comes to discussing greatness.

Benaud was a highly successful captain. He has an imposing winning record, which is the most important criterion. He is also famed for having started the habit of throwing the Australian dressing room wide open to every person who wants to get the lowdown on the latest personal interest story, with which to regale the supposedly news-hungry public about the goings on of their cricket heroes. Benaud is remembered too, with mixed feelings, as the captain who started the rush to hug the player who had just brought off a catch or managed to hit the stumps with a smart return.

Bob Simpson's captaincy performances did not do justice to his ability. He suffered from the same complaint as Collins and Johnson – he lacked a pair of great bowlers.

Bill Lawry was next, axed for the very same reason as his fellow Victorian Jack Ryder in 1930 – not a match-winning bowler in his side.

Then of course came Ian Chappell, who made a name for himself that looks likely to last for a good few years to come. Chappell's appointment as national captain and Dennis Lillee's very first appearance in a Test took place almost simultaneously. Lillee went on to become the greatest Test wicket-taker of all time and Chappell's leadership reputation grew commensurately. To give Chappell further grounds for stardom, Jeff Thomson and Max Walker were ushered into the ring to make a Test bowling splash sufficient to drown any further discussion.

Greg Chappell took over where his brother left off, but his star, and Australia's, waned as our bowling stars aged. Recently of course we have had the West Indies completely dominating the game, and you don't need a tertiary education to know why. Their record-breaking sequence was finally brought to an end last summer, the summer of 1984-85, because a pair of Australian bowlers, Bob Holland and Murray Bennett, took complete charge of the fifth Test in Sydney. Allan Border is probably modest enough to regard himself as very fortunate that the Australian selectors finally got round to picking Holland and Bennett to bowl in tandem on that Sydney wicket.

Kim Hughes was not so lucky. He did all the things which you could ask of a captain, which in my cynical view of the subject consists mainly of writing down the batting order and changing the field around occasionally to let the crowd know you are in charge. Like just about everybody I spoke to at the time, I felt very sorry for Hughes, and I am sure he finally paid the penalty for not joining the rebellion of 1977. This 'misdemeanour' left a legacy of hostility from people who should have known, and behaved, better. Australia would have won the final Test on the 1984-85 season just as comfortably if Kim Hughes had been captain. If he had had a little more constructive support and a little less criticism he would still be firmly ensconced as Australia's captain today.

No wonder I find continued cause to refer to my faithful old collie dog, who sits by my side in pensive mood whenever I take up my pen to write about the ups and downs of Australian captains. There are many more of them still to come to strut their stuff. They will all, at the end, agree entirely with me that it is bowlers, or the lack of them, which will make or break their reputation.

22 Internal Strife

Gubby Allen's 1936-37 England team was a very different kettle of fish from Jardine's side. There was not a hint of unpleasantness during the battles on the field. The main irritations as far as the Australians were concerned were internal ones, but more of that later.

Without Sutcliffe, Hendren, Paynter, and of course Larwood, they did not look to be a particularly strong side, but they outplayed us in the first two Tests, in Sydney and Brisbane, where they also had the good luck to catch us on wet wickets. In Brisbane we needed 380 to win in the fourth innings, which was a pretty tall order anyway, but the rain settled our chances and we were all out for 58. In the Sydney Test England were 426 for 6, Hammond not out 231, when it rained. We batted after a thunderstorm, and made 80, O'Reilly not out 37. I got something like my money's worth that day because the Wolffe's Schnapps people paid us £5 ($10) for every six, and one of the cigarette firms paid £50 to anyone who hit three sixes in an innings, which I had done.

In the third Test England were caught on a wet wicket in their first innings and made only 76, Hammond making a courageous 32 in almost impossible conditions. We made 564 in our second innings, when Fingleton (136) and Bradman (270) put on 346 for the fifth wicket. England never looked like getting the runs. In Adelaide, the fourth Test, Australia made 288 and England 330 in the first innings. Then we made 433 in the second innings – Bradman 212. At one stage, with Hammond batting well, it looked as if England might get the runs to win the series, but Fleetwood-Smith bowled Hammond with an unplayable ball and went on to take 6 wickets, so the series was all square with one Test to play.

Because the series was so close, and because so many people were interested in cricket in those days, we were getting huge crowds everywhere we went. On the third day of the final Test, in Melbourne, 87,000 came to the game, a record which stood until the 1960-61 series against the West Indies, by which time the capacity of the ground had been considerably increased. Attendances for that final Test was 350,000 and for the whole series was 943,000, and both of those records still stand.

They got their money's worth in Melbourne. Bradman made 169, and with McCabe (112) put on 250 runs in under three hours. Badcock made 118 and our total was 604. We bowled the Englishmen out for 239 and 165, and I took 5 wickets in the first innings and 3 in the second.

So I suppose it was an exciting series, although for many of us in the Australian team it was not a particularly happy one. Many irritating 'rubs' were experienced in Australian cricket in those later years of the 'thirties, and I was certainly involved in my fair share of them.

The first of them came to light in Brisbane before the first Test of the 1936-37 series began.

Stan McCabe, recently married, had arranged for his wife to fly to Brisbane in a light aircraft on the opening day, but he was mortified when the secretary of the Queensland Cricket Association informed him that there would be no ticket available for her to be given a seat in the main grandstand. Three or four of us hurriedly decided that the situation demanded an immediate stern reaction. Don Bradman, the new captain, was informed that he would have great difficulty in finding a quorum to accompany him to the middle of the 'Gabba if he happened to lose the toss to Gubby Allen that morning. The ticket arrangement was hastily amended and our team gave the little plane a reassuring wave from the field as it dipped its wings over the ground on its way across to the

Brisbane airport. That incident left nasty tastes in our mouths and quite obviously some official palates were also offended.

Then, during the second Test in Sydney, our second heavy defeat because of rain, a schoolmate from my Marengo days who was an employee of the Post Office at the Sydney Cricket Ground took time off to come to the Australian dressing room door to give me the interesting news that I was apparently in trouble with officialdom. He said that urgent telegrams on the subject had been flowing through the wires.

When that match finished a few of us went to lunch at the old Metropole Hotel in Bridge Street, where I noticed our captain Don Bradman and a Melbourne journalist named Major dining at another table. I took the opportunity of asking Don if he could give me any information about the trouble that was brewing. He knew nothing of it whatever.

It all came to a head at the end of the third Test in Melbourne. Stan McCrabe, Chuck Fleetwood-Smith, Leo O'Brien and I were told to attend the Victorian Cricket Association rooms on the afternoon the match finished, to meet the members of the Australian Board of Control.

None of us had a clue what it was about. No one else in the team knew anything. Bradman himself knew nothing about it.

There were just the four of us, four Irishmen – to this day I don't know why Fingleton didn't get a guernsey – and we went along to the VCA without any idea of what the Board of Control was cooking up. Frankly, I still don't know. There were four of them there that I can remember: Roger Hartigan, Harry Hodgetts, Dr Alan Robertson and Dr Ramsay Mailer, a Collins Street specialist. They all seemed very uneasy about the proceedings. After a few embarrassed preliminaries Dr Robertson began to read from what looked like a longish typed statement, to the effect that they believed some members of the Board felt that some members of the team were indulging in too much beer, and not enough physical fitness and team spirit. Insurbordination was also mentioned.

We seemed an unlikely crew to be levelling those charges at. McCabe had top-scored for Australia in the second innings of the second Test and the first innings of the third Test, and had in fact captained Australia in the field on the final day of the third Test, which we won, when Bradman was down with a heavy cold. Fleetwood-Smith it must be said was an unusual character, given to whistling as he ran in to bowl and imitating bird calls in the field. He and I had actually been called upon to open Australia's second innings of the third Test, when the pitch was wet and dangerous. Neither of us troubled the scorer, but Chuck did manage to face 26 balls without getting the bat on any of them, before snicking the 27th, from Voce, to Verity at slip. This was his first Test in the series and he had taken 5 English wickets in the second innings. Personally, I would have regarded as ill-founded any inference that I did not always give one hundred per cent in the field.

So there we were, accused, it seemed, as representatives of an insubordinate and disloyal team of slackers and boozers. It was more than I could take. I begged Dr Robertson's pardon for interrupting, and asked whether we four were being held responsible.

The answer was, 'No.'

What, then, were we there for? The answer was not provided.

The meeting broke up in general confusion and further mutual embarrassment with most of the typed statement unread.

That may appear to be one of the stranger unresolved episodes in the annals of the official side of the game, but I was later involved in another equally puzzling incident which caused me no little unhappiness and lessened my respect for officialdom.

It occurred when I attended the medical examination to testify to my fitness for the 1938 touring team to England. Along with the other New South Wales members of the side I lined up at the designated Macquarie Street surgery, where I was informed that there was sugar in my specimen. I was told that a sugar test would be arranged with a specialist in that field for the next day, and for good measure, that if it went against me I would not go to England.

When I told my team-mates that I was an unlikely candidate for the tour their first reaction was to laugh raucously.

'You unfit! Baloney!' was their reaction.

In self-defence I decided to drive out to Kensington to see a medico friend who had been an outstanding cricketer, and I asked him to bung me through all the sugar tests known to his profession. He put me through four of them and came up with a negative reaction in each. The next day I passed the official test.

I was fit, but I was suspicious, and subsequently two chance remarks gave me cause to believe that there had been a clandestine set-up to take the wind out of my sails. The first remark was made in England during the 1938 tour. The Duke of Portland invited a few of us to accompany him to the sideboard bar at his Welback Abbey home in Sherwood Forest whilst the less favoured members of the side went for a bus ride of inspection round the historic sites on the vast estate. Our manager, Bill Jeanes, who had not been invited to the imbibing board, sidled up to me saying, 'I'd go on the bus if I were you, Bill. Remember the trouble with your medical test back home.' I gave Bill the benefit of a few well chosen words, and I, not he, leaned comfortably against the bar.

The other occasion was years later, in 1946-47, and it came after Sid Barnes had jumped the turnstile to get into the Melbourne Cricket Ground to take part in the third Test of that series. He too had had an interview with Dr Robertson after the incident. I saw him later, and the first thing he said to me was, 'You never told me you had diabetes.'

I never had it explained to me how it happened that my name came up for discussion, but having a first-hand knowledge of the extent of Sid's arguments in self-defence, I realized that the old 'Doc' had dropped his guard surprisingly.

The other business from those years which still riles me is the omission of Clarrie Grimmett from Australian teams after the tour to South Africa in 1935-36.

On that delightful trip in which we made history by playing a full-scale programme of five Tests, Grimmett and I accounted for 71 of the 98 South African wickets to fall in the Tests. Grimmett's share was a record-breaking 44 wickets collected at the rate of 14.59 runs each. Between the two of us we were responsible for 187 of the 289 victims falling to the eleven bowlers who got their arms over in the sixteen matches played on tour.

Grimmett returned to Australia at the end of that tour, towards the end of March in 1936, to find that he not only had a new State captain in Don Bradman, but also a brand new contender for his spinner's place in the South Australian side. This was Frank Ward, who has played some of his early club cricket as a member of the Sydney St George Club, to which the youthful Bradman had first transferred his allegiance on leaving Bowral.

To the utter dismay of all who knew him and admired his wonderful skill, Clarrie sank with incredible speed into cricket's graveyard. He failed to gain a place in the Australian line-up to meet Gubby Allen's team on tour here in 1936-37, making way for Ward who in my honest opinion was rewarded far beyond his rightful claims. Ward played in the first three Tests, and took 11 wickets at an average of 39, the worst average of the Australian bowlers. He was then picked for the 1938 tour of England where he bowled thirty overs for 142 runs without taking a wicket in the one Test in which he was selected.

Before that team was chosen for England, Bradman invited me to pick him up at his Sydney hotel en route to the Sydney Cricket Ground during the course of a Sheffield Shield match being played between New South Wales and South Australia. Such a request, quite unusual, raised my eyebrows and my curiosity. I looked forward to discovering the plum in the pie. I was less than pleased when I learned that Bradman merely wanted to find out my personal reaction to the question, 'Who was the better bowler – Grimmett or Ward?'

I left him in no doubt of my opinion, although I thought it a ridiculous pastime even to ponder the question. I did draw the captain-selector's notice to Ward's reaction to the manhandling he received from the English batsman Charlie Barnett in the first Test of the 1936-37 series.

I can still see it happening and I still find it hard to believe. Fielding at point, at first I looked on admiringly as the leg spinner bowled splendidly to the aggressive opener from Gloucestershire. Barnett loved to move his feet forward – he hated being forced back. From my prize viewing position I admired the way in which Ward was teasing the fleet-footed Englishman down the pitch and I eagerly anticipated the stumping chance that would inevitably arrive in 'Cracker' Oldfield's gloves. Ward finally beat him with flight. But Barnett was no blushing schoolboy caught unawares in the apple orchard. He knew his business: 'When in real trouble hit with all your might,' was the timeworn axiom that Barnett knew best of all. Completely wrong-footed, off balance, and beautifully set up for the kill, Barnett gave it the lot, and hit the ball clean over the players' dressing room and out of the 'Gabba.

That was the last ball Ward pitched up during the day.

I used the incident, and I made much of it – to no avail. Poor old Clarrie missed the bus and we all paid for it. It is not fair, I suppose, to rub it in – one should try to avoid it perhaps – but Grimmett himself rubbed it in very effectively in the Australian season after the '38 tour in collecting 72 victims in the domestic season to establish an Australian record.

Too old! Nuts! The simple fact is that Grimmett established himself as the best bowler in the world in South Africa in 1935-36, but he was left out of the Australian Test team in 1936-37 and in 1938. For me, Grimmett's omission from the 1938 English tour goes down as the most biased, ill-considered piece of selection known to Australian cricket. You will have to excuse the strength of that statement, but Grimmett's absence made my own tour in 1938 a litany of frustrated endeavour.

Ward simply never made the grade in the big-time. Fleetwood-Smith, brilliant as he was and capable of dismissing any batsman – I've never seen a spin bowler with as much ability – didn't have the consistency necessary to wear a good batsman down. He could not bowl tight for long periods, and as a result the opposition could keep the score going along.

With my partner, tried, true, and eminently reliable, back home twiddling his spinning fingers in Adelaide, I tried to carry two spinners who never at any stage looked like shouldering the weight that Grimmett accepted and shouldered wholeheartedly every time the ball was thrown to him. It was an unpardonable error on the part of the three-man selection committee to which Don Bradman had recently been appointed. I have always suspected that Bradman himself was the guiding hand in the dropping of Grimmett.

Everything seemed to point in that direction. If I am right then this dreadful error must go down as a substantial chink in the shining armour of the great batsman-captain. To me it will always appear to have been an outstanding incongruity that this batting genius could be held instrumental in the passing of a bowling genius of equal dimension to his own.

23 England 1938

By now you may have the impression that some of the joy had gone out of the game for me. My baptism in the bodyline series and the later breaks with officialdom had corrected many of my youthful illusions.

I did not look forward to the 1938 tour of England with the eager anticipation of younger days. You can take it from me that cricket quickly ceases to be fun once you have settled into the round eternal of six days' cricket per week through a four-and-a-half months' tour. As you rise from the couch each morning you eventually find yourself saying, 'Oh God! Not another day's cricket.' I said that so many times that I wonder now to myself why I even bothered to go back to have a second serving of the treatment. In the end it is only the camaraderie of the team, the lifelong friendships which you forge, and the opportunity for interesting sorties outside the grind of the cricket grounds which make the experience worthwhile.

There are perhaps half a dozen things which stand out in my mind from that 1938 tour, which, if it wasn't my happiest touring experience, still produced some very good cricket and some history-making performances.

We soon realized that, despite the absence of Grimmett, the Englishmen had taken precautions to prevent the Australian spin bowlers from dominating the series. The wicket for the first Test at Trent Bridge was made to last for ever. I opened the bowling with Ernie McCormick and England's opening pair of Charlie Barnett and Len Hutton each took the opportunity to score a century. Eddie Paynter made 216 not out and Denis Compton also made a hundred.

England declared at 8 for 658 and we had lost 2 for 111 when Stan McCabe came in to play the third of his immortal innings. Wickets fell steadily and with 6 men out for 194 we faced virtually certain defeat. With Ben Barnett, McCabe took the score to 263, and when Barnett went he really cut loose, scoring 127 of the 148 runs made in the final 80 minutes of the innings. He did exactly as he liked against an attack which included Ken Farnes and Doug Wright, two very good bowlers. He took runs off nearly every ball he faced in the last 80 minutes, and continually trumped Hammond's efforts to keep him away from the strike.

It was of this innings that Don Bradman himself said, 'You may never see its like again,' and when McCabe came out Bradman said to him, 'I'd have given a great deal to have played an innings like that one.'

We made 411 and although we had to follow on Bradman and Bill Brown made patient centuries in the second innings and we drew the game quite comfortably.

At Lord's England won the toss again and made 494, with Hammond playing his last great innings for a majestic 240. Bill Brown then batted right through the Australian innings. I gave him some help in the tail, hitting a couple of sixes in scoring 42, and he was 206 not out when our last wicket fell. That game was drawn too, with Bradman scoring a hundred in our second innings.

The Manchester Test was completely washed out and all the wet weather they were having apparently interfered with the preparation of the wicket for the scheduled fourth Test, because at last we got a wicket you could do something on. England won the toss and batted. Fleetwood-Smith took 3 wickets and I took 5, only Hammond (76) played with any authority, and we got them all out for 223. We then made 242 with Bradman (103) playing a really good innings in poor light on a difficult pitch and against hree really good bowlers in those conditions, Bowes, Verity and

Wright. Although the Englishmen apparently did not share our view, we Australians regarded the leg spinner Doug Wright as the best bowler in England at the time, and we felt we were lucky in that if he had had more bowling in the second and third Tests the results might well have been different.

There are those who say Bradman was not at his best when the wicket wasn't good. Well of course no batsman is, but anyone who saw his innings that day would have no doubts about his ability when conditions were against him. Fleetwood-Smith and I got 4 and 5 wickets respectively and England were all out for 123 in the second innings. Although we only needed a little over 100 we had a struggle and a race against the rain before we won the game with 5 wickets in hand. Hassett, dropped early, finally settled the issue with some judicious hitting.

So then we lined up at the Oval for the decider, and you could smell the cow dung a mile away. There was no way that our spinners were going to win the game for us on that pitch. It was dosed to the eyeballs.

Hammond won the toss for the fourth time in the series, and the rest is history, although it should be related that Hutton was missed twice, off McCabe and Fleetwood-Smith, before he was 50. He was out there for over 13 hours, and for sheer dedication, concentration, and relentlessness of purpose his 364 was as good an innings as I have ever seen. Leyland and Hardstaff made big scores too. England declared at 7 for 903, and with Bradman and Fingleton both injured in the field and unable to bat, we could only muster 201 and 123.

The Test series was squared. With our team decimated as a result of our annihilation at the Oval, we had to cope with the final matches of a long and tiring tour.

Don Bradman had been lost to us for the rest of the tour before making an appearance with the bat in the fifth Test. He had put himself on to bowl, but during his third over landed a foot in a deep hole that I had dug with the heel of my left boot in the course of delivering the 85 overs which was my contribution to the carnival spirit. His ankle was badly sprained and he was carried from the field where he joined Jack Fingleton who had also retired from the fray with a leg muscle injury. To make matters worse Lindsay Hassett was making spasmodic references to a broken bone in his left hand, but as he was merely a 'walking wounded' nobody was prepared to give him a hearing at all.

Hassett sportingly saddled up for three of the six fixtures which followed the Oval defeat. Despite his painful injury he went in at number three at Hove against Sussex and scored 74 and 56 in a drawn match, and he played against England XIs in festival games at Blackpool and Folkestone before his hand took him out of the tour permanently.

Our second 'keeper, the late Charlie Walker, who lost his life whilst serving with the RAAF a few years later, had been continually out of action through finger injuries. Indeed he played in only nine first-class games on tour. Ben Barnett had twenty-two games, and was forced to carry on unspelled for the remainder of the tour. With three games remaining we found ourselves without even a twelfth man, and the effort being put up by our gallant wicketkeeper was clear to everybody. Taking into account that Barnett had stood up to the 2013 deliveries sent down by his bowlers in the fifth Test and had then gone on to take every remaining delivery until the tour programme concluded on Trinity College ground in Dublin four weeks later, you will realize why I think his effort was one of the bravest performances I have witnessed on a long tour, the itinerary for which we Australians rather thought must have been laid out by an undertaker.

After the Sussex game we went north to Blackpool, then back down south to Folkestone, after which we made our way up north again to play another All England XI at Scarborough, where a team led by Bob Wyatt gave us a ten wicket beating. By then we were wondering what was meant by the word 'festival'. Who was supposed to be having fun? Fortunately, no temperamental performers showed up in what was left of the team – some were even able to glean some humour from the whole shemozzle.

As a final note on that tour I should tell you that one night in a London Club I had the good manners to listen quietly to two young men discussing the relative importance cricket-wise of Bradman's world record Test score of 334 put up at Leeds in 1930, and that of the 364 with which Hutton had broken it at the Oval. The consensus arrived at was that as Bradman had faced the cream of English bowling, he must take precedence over the Yorkshire lad Hutton, who 'had nothing really to contend with.'

Acting captain Stan McCabe, filling in permanently for the injured Bradman, had precisely the right disposition to take his team calmly through the crisis conditions. With his ready smile, soft voice, twinkling eyes and his immense courage he performed a triumph in leading that jaded team over some of the stoniest ridges an Australian team has negotiated.

It was the Irish section of the campaign that restored our feelings, and made life worthwhile. Crossing England once more we took ship from Heysham, bound for Belfast, and after a game in Northern Ireland we set out eagerly for the south, which is where, as I trust you will recall, it all began.

24 Six of the Best

As I have said before, what really makes cricket worthwhile is the experiences you have and the people you meet off the field. I have made many lifelong friends and been involved with some great characters through the game.

JACK CHEGWYN

I have not always seen eye to eye with the game's administrators, but John W. (Cheggy) Chegwyn is one administrator who has my wholehearted admiration, and whose contribution to the game over a quarter of a century would be nearly impossible to better.

Cheggy has been a cricket fanatic since his school days at Botany Primary and his long sojourn at Sydney Grammar. On leaving school, where he earned a solid reputation as one of Grammar's outstandingly gifted batsmen, Jack made his way down to the Randwick District Cricket Club at Coogee Oval, to give that famous old team his solid support for the remainder of his cricket life.

The fact that he gave twenty-four years of his time to the responsibilities of selecting his State's representatives in all first-class cricket during that lengthy period has never counted half so importantly with me as the magnificent work he carried out in fostering this State's bush talent. Cheggy started his famous campaign, aimed at country centres, in 1939 and continued doing it for just on forty years. Every New South Wales town with any rating at all in cricket organization and enthusiasm has tales to tell of Cheggy's initiative. He even ventured into the realms of international cricket in 1952, when he took his band to Hong Kong and invited me to lead it.

Probably not many people remember that Jack scored a very important century for New South Wales in Adelaide in the late 1930s, and what makes it most impressive is that he had to deal with the wiles of one of Australia's most celebrated spin bowlers, Clarrie Grimmett, in doing so. I saw that performance, and had good cause for admiring the skills he showed, for the simple reason that I myself was leading New South Wales in the match, in the absence of Stan McCabe.

Cheggy's career as a country cricket entrepreneur began soon after McCabe and I returned from the 1938 Australian cricket tour of England. The two of us were continually receiving invitations to take city teams to perform in the bush. We were both products of country cricket, and were keen to help in whatever way we could. We hit upon the brilliant idea of asking our mate Cheggy to try his hand at organizing a tour for us. Once he indicated that the idea was attractive to him we made absolutely certain that every invitation we got was directed straight into his capable hands. He went for it like a duck to water, and in very quick time country centres aimed their pleas to him. To my certain knowledge he kept them thoroughly satisfied year after year.

His first trip was to Canberra late in 1939. He chose his own team, with McCabe and myself as his strike power. From the very first day he kept the little black book for which he became famous, and every relevant detail of every subsequent tour was documented in those books. So far as I know no one has ever had a chance to read them. At home in Banksia Street, Botany, he and his wife Shirley are presiding over a collection of little black books which surely represents a fabulously interesting part of New South Wales cricket history. Anyone writing the story of Australian cricket over the middle portion of the twentieth century can be quite sure that he will be missing enormously relevant resources if he fails to make use of Jack Chegwyn's treasured little books.

Cheggy started his campaign on solid lines. He made certain that he took three or four top-line players upon whom he could rely, not only to prevent his team from being outplayed by the bushwhackers, but also to provide the inspiration for talented country boys keen to learn by example. To add weight to the team he carefully chose two or three promising city colts whom he knew would profit by an opportunity to brush shoulders with team-mates whose names had already become famous. Having attended to the backbone of a team along those thoughtful lines, Cheggy was able to pick his social members. This was a wonderful idea. These were players who, apart from possessing white pants and buckskin boots, supplied the brand of good fellowship that Cheggy knew was always tremendously popular with his country hosts.

Seldom, in his early years, did Chegwyn venture forth without the support of our great mate Algie Wright from Marrickville, who carried his weight, all eighteen stone of it, by dispensing a brand of bonhomie which kept everyone within earshot glad to be alive and kicking. Others who never failed to contribute tremendously to this highly important section of the Chegwyn campaign were the young Sydney barrister Wally South, who had played an important batting role with Sydney University during his studentship, and the elongated speed bowler from North Sydney, Peter Cahill, who was an hilarious integral part of the incongruous duo he formed with the corpulent Algie.

One rule made at the very start was that every member must pull his weight socially by being easy to get on with both on and off the field, and a cardinal obligation to every member of the side was that tales must never be told out of school. It was certain that a wagging tongue applied loosely in recounting touring tales back home was the surest method of making a player quite certain he would never again be invited to tour with Jack Chegwyn. They were magnificent conditions of employment, and Cheggy's teams during those forty years were joyously accepted throughout the length and breadth of New South Wales.

There is no need to go into the details of Chegwyn's successes with country cricket. One has only to cast an eye down the list of country players who were able to show their wares to city selectors during the years of the Chegwyn reign. His contribution was entirely practical, although there was never a hint that he did the job for any other reason than that he loved it.

DR ROWLEY POPE

In a recent cricket publication I was devastated to see an historical picture of an Australian touring team shown with the names of all the players accurately placed in the right positions, but a blank with the word 'unknown' shown in brackets beneath the photograph of every Australian cricket tourist's distinguished friend and helpmate, Doctor Rowley Pope.

Right from the 1890s, when his medical studies in England had been finalized, Rowley devoted his life to cricket. Medicine was but a sideline which helped his conscience to assure him that he was pulling his weight as a tourist.

Born with a silver spoon in his mouth, as we used to say, Rowley was a classic Australian. His loyalty and concern for our welfare never faltered. When Charlie Walker, the 1938 support wicketkeeper, dared to buy a red and gold look-alike MCC tie, the grand old man told him off in no uncertain terms – such conduct was unacceptable amongst the right people, he said – but he did it ever so quietly, to ensure that Charlie was not embarrassed.

It was the usual thing for Rowley to pack and cart along with him on tour thirty to forty suitcases, the contents of each all itemized and recorded in a filing system kept in an inside pocket. It seemed there was nothing that a trip to his cabin could fail to produce.

Cracker Oldfield, on board the *Orford* in 1934 somewhere mid-stream in the Indian Ocean, complained to our medico friend that he had lost the tiny screw that moored the earpiece to his sunglasses. Rowley returned from the resulting visit to his trunks with three different screws, from which he asked Cracker to take his pick.

Farmers Ltd of Sydney, now gone to glory, had the right to claim relationship with him. He was, presumably, a big shareholder therein. His brother 'Park' was one of that firm's top executives and Rowley was their plenipotentiary at large. He had fairly large investments in New Guinea gold, and when that commodity took a surprising turn upwards in 1934, over a bottle of champagne which he had purchased for celebrative purposes in one of those bleak North England hotels, Rowley advised us all that we must never – repeat, never – invest our money underground. I did not fully understand the reason for that warning: I suppose he must have had to wait a long time for it to come good. But we enjoyed the champagne, and we heeded the advice – not that there was much likelihood of an Australian cricketer plunging into the mining industry in those days.

He was a great stickler for the right way to do things: to pour a bottle of wine, to serve a cup of tea, to be a good listener. Few of the team enjoyed dining with the old man, who had been presiding over touring cricket tables for more than forty years. He was exceedingly rough on the waiters or waitresses, using language so curt and peremptory that most of us were embarrassed. Then, having demanded and received the best possible service from the sorely tried servant, he would mark the occasion by handing over an enormous tip. Quite often I considered the possibility of donning a white coat and setting to work at Rowley's table, but I doubt I had the temperament to accept all that went with it, save the tip.

Rowley had once played cricket for Australia, a fact which he jealously withheld from all but the players whom he knew he could trust. Should you take the trouble to peruse the scores of matches played back in the 1880s you will discover that one R. J. Pope had two innings in a Melbourne Test, but gave the scorers very little to do.

It happened, so he told me in great secrecy, because of a dispute among the Australian players over match fees. He filled in a few times for Australian teams on tour in England too, although he was not a chosen member of the touring parties. I suppose such an event was quite possible when teams of twelve men had the temerity to attempt months-long tours of England. Anyhow his Test career was short-lived, but you can take it from me that no player had a longer, more successful, or more enjoyable first-class career than Roland J. Pope.

I do hope that the publication referred to, should it face the barrier for a reprint, acknowledges the presence of a very great Australian cricket tourist in that photographic line-up.

HANS EBELING

Don Bradman and I had our baptism in big cricket in a match for New South Wales Second XI against the Victorian Second XI at the Sydney Cricket Ground on 1 January 1927.

Victoria's opening bowler in that match was a tall, rather burly, fast-medium swing bowler who ran in from about fifteen paces, directed his stock-in-trade outswinger accurately at the middle and off stumps, and concentrated purposefully on bringing his three slips fieldsmen into profitable play.

His only success for the match appeared in the scorebook as Bradman b Ebeling 43.

That impressed nobody at the time. Certainly not the Victorian selectors who gave him no other opportunity that season. Nobody had heard of Bradman then, he was just a country kid whom the foraging New South Wales selectors had run across in the wilds of the Southern Uplands.

Ebeling did not bowl Bradman, let me hasten to tell you. Had he done so Hans would never have let me forget that he had done much more impressively in his first encounter with the boy wonder than I had done. Bradman, who had started slowly and had gone on to show glimpses of extraordinary batting talent, got himself out. In stepping well back to force a good length ball on his leg stump through mid-wicket, he committed the cardinal error of stepping onto his stumps just as he made the contact which sent the ball flying to the boundary.

Bradman went back to Bowral and Ebeling to Melbourne after that meeting, both to wait some time for the next invitation. I thought I was the lucky one of the trio when I was asked to take part in a Testimonal match for Charles Macartney at the Sydney Cricket Ground in February, but I soon discovered how my luck was shaping up when my employer, the New South Wales Education Department, informed me that the unshakeable rule for leave was 'representing State or Country'.

Ebeling had one Sheffield Shield match for Victoria in the

following season and then a full-scale Shield season in 1928-29, during which he took 19 wickets – a highly creditable performance, remembering that there were then only four teams in the competition. It was during that season that Bradman and Ebeling met once again on the Sydney Cricket Ground, where I saw them as a spectator from the Hill. Bradman scored 340 not out to break William Murdoch's 1881-82 Sydney Cricket Ground record for the highest score on the local ground.

Just as Ebeling had shown convincingly that he was Test material, his Melbourne employers informed him that the time had come when he had to choose between cricket and his career in commerce. There were few employers those days who could afford to carry anyone who constantly sought leave for sport. Few people indeed received the privilege of annual holidays. Unless a young man was lucky enough to find a job in which proficiency at cricket was likely to be regarded as a commercial asset, it was best for him to forget about his sport and concentrate on the serious job of earning his living.

So Ebeling quietly walked out of first-class cricket altogether. However, in keeping with the old adage, 'you can't keep a good man down', he blasted his way back into the very top line of Australian cricket in two matches played in mid-November 1933, when he had arranged a fortnight's furlough from his shipping company job.

Chosen to play in the Blackie-Ironmonger Testimonial match which started at the MCG in November 1933, Ebeling, playing for Victor Richardson's side against Bill Woodfull's XI, made an enormous impression when he collected five wickets for 72 runs off 27 overs. He really should have had six wickets. In the opening overs I missed a real 'sitter' from the broad bat of Bill Ponsford. That fielding error took a long time to be forgotten, but I don't regret it, because I am certain that it was the means by which our lifelong friendship began.

Another event which sticks vividly in my memory of that historic day in Ebeling's career on his beloved MCG, was that his inseparable mate, the six-feet-six-inch Lisle Nagel, fielding beside me at first slip, ricked his neck badly as he turned to carry on a short conversation about my fielding misdemeanour. He left the field as a result of it, and that incident brought his great bowling career to an end.

Nagel was a resourceful, fast-medium right-hander capable of getting wickets in any company. He could take the new ball into the wind and swing it either way, could bring it back off the pitch at times quite surprisingly, and, this above all, he had the best 'quicky' of the day. Even the country's top line batsmen were forever on sharp lookout for that Nagel blockbuster. I have often wondered at the strange whims of fate when I think that at the time Australia was suffering the blow of losing the gifted Nagel, another great bowler was on the boil at the other end in the shape of Hans Ebeling, who certainly loomed up on the Test horizon that morning.

Ebeling toured England with Bill Woodfull's team in 1934 and was, luckily for me, my constant companion throughout. Starting with a wicket from the first ball he bowled in England, he performed so thoroughly well throughout that the English batsman Jack Hobbs classed him as one of the best bowlers he had met. Off the field he was a splendid example to all – a wonderful mixer, holding his own with distinction in all the social commitments of the team. At Windsor Castle he succeeded in keeping Queen Mary deeply interested in some trivial topic of conversation for a good length of time, in a scene which was just as interesting to me in the viewing of it, as it was to the Queen's hearing. None but a very gallant, highly self-assured young man would have dared engage Her Majesty in trivial conversation. She had an air which gave little incentive to any but the bravest social performer.

Ebeling's career in cricket was disappointingly short. Back from England, he rejected an invitation to tour South Africa so that he could concentrate fully on a new job he had taken with an international oil company. Yet he did manage to take over the Victorian captaincy vacated by Bill Woodful, and to lead Victoria to Shield victories in 1934-35 and 1936-37, not a bad record for a member of the bowling fraternity, which has always been regarded as too thick in the head to rise successfully to the giddy heights of captaincy.

As captain, most good judges thought, Ebeling got far more value out of the left-arm spinner Fleetwood-Smith than anyone else could. He knew that in Fleetwood-Smith he was being privileged to handle one of the world's most gifted players, and he adopted the attitude that it was his duty to get the last ounce of skill out of him. His motto in this respect was, 'Don't ask him, tell him', and every Victorian player of that time will tell you that Chuck responded to the treatment so well that he was able to give full scope to his extraordinary ability.

At the end of his career – some say the end was brought about by it – Ebeling was involved in a couple of scraps with Bradman, then the South Australian captain. In Melbourne on one occasion Bradman was noticeably unsettled by a brilliant and aggressive exhibition of new ball bowling from Ernie McCormick, and looked complainingly to captain Ebeling. The upshot was that Hans advised The Don, 'You run your side, I'll run mine.' Ernie McCormick, who for three or four overs was quite as dangerous as any fast bowler I have seen, was later described by Bradman, in a speech at the Savoy Hotel in London in 1938, as the fastest bowler in the world.

After his retirement from first-class cricket Hans Ebeling immersed himself in the affairs of his beloved Melbourne Cricket Ground, and later became, for too short a time before his death in 1980, its president.

It was his idea in the first place that the famous Melbourne Cricket Club should stage the Centenary Test, an historic event which they handled with such infinite pride and flair that it has come to be regarded as the classic cricket social event of the century.

CLARRIE GRIMMETT

Clarence Victor Grimmett, my treasured bowling partner, who was perhaps as much responsible for my success as I was, was born in New Zealand's Dunedin and spent all his boyhood years in the Shaky Isles. As a schoolboy he harboured ideas of succeeding in cricket, the game he loved, as a fast bowler. (I never cease to wonder why it is that every ambitious boy with his mind set on cricket starts with the idea of developing his speed. Perhaps it is the primitive appeal of violence, a hangover from the Stone Age, when strength of arm was very much more important than the supremacy of mind over muscle.)

Fortunately for cricket history, especially Australia's, a North Island schoolmaster decided that young Grimmett's prospects were much brighter as a spinner. He began to concentrate on leg spin and to think it all out with the supreme self-confidence that never forsook him throughout his life. No cricketer I knew thought half so clearly about his cricket as did Grimmett. I'm prepared to bet that he never let the game slip far from his mind, even in the depths of winter. He was forever thinking of ways and means of *Tricking the Batsman*, which was the title of a book he released at one stage of his career, and which he found to his dismay bounced back upon him from time to time: quite often we heard a well-meaning barracker calling, 'You'd better read your book, Clarrie', especially when our arch opponent, the wonderfully gifted English batsman Walter Hammond, was in full cry.

Grimmett absolutely amazed me with the scope of his research into the skills of the game. He had a theory for everything, and generally speaking he was so very close to the bone in all of it that one dared not argue with him unless one was fully prepared. He knew all there was to know about fielding in the covers, a position where he shone without any show of flamboyance. Never once did I see him dive headlong at a cover drive: there was no need for him to do so, he seemed always to have sufficient time to get to the ball on two feet and take it in two hands.

His batting was a constant source of pride. He so fancied himself as a batsman that whenever I appeared at the crease with him he always assumed the fatherly role of farming the strike away from me. I often resented it of course, and took a sly pleasure out of running him out in the Leeds Test in 1934. He had backed up much too adventurously, but he never forgot it. He spoke of my misdemeanour with haughty disdain every time we met and talked of days gone by.

Our approaches to bowling of the so-called 'express' variety were fundamentally similar – we both took a quick preliminary step away from the line of flight – but of course so far as Clarrie was concerned we had entirely different objectives in mind. Mine, he always said, was to get me right out of harm's way. He was entirely right, a fact which I admit quite readily. Grimmett's explanation for his own celerity in doing exactly the same thing was that it gave him the opportunity to indulge his great facility with the back cut. His team-mates, who along with me doted on him, never thought a Grimmett innings was worth watching unless it began with a brilliantly executed back cut. It was his masterpiece, and it was probably also the best face-saving shot the game has produced.

It was as a batsman that I first laid my schoolboy's eyes on C. V. Grimmett. The Victorian Sheffield Shield team, returning from the inaugural post-World War I match with New South Wales in Sydney in 1919, delighted the Goulburn district when they graciously agreed to show the cricket flag on the local sports ground.

Having read the press 'blurb' about the slow right-handed leg spinner, I was surprised to find him opening the batting with the team's manager, Matt Ellis. I often told him, years later, that it was the only time in my life that I held the opinion that he must have been a good batsman. He must have been good, I thought, to accompany the manager to the crease ahead of men like Vernon Ransford, Edgar Mayne, Jack Ryder, Les Keating, Basil Onyons and Phil Le Couteur.

When his name went up on the miniature makeshift scoreboard (of which I felt inordinately proud for the very good reason that I had never seen a scoreboard before) the local lads misspelt it 'Grummett'. From that time onward he was Grummett to me, a term which was abbreviated to 'Grum', and which all his friends eventually used as a term of endearment and unbounded respect.

'Grum' got 38 in painfully slow time before he was caught and bowled by the local champion, George Tickner. He did however impress me with his dexterity in getting the ball away through the slips, with a shot which at that time I had only associated with the name of Alan Kippax.

Clarrie's reign with the Victorian team was short-lived. Only twice was he chosen for the State, though he lived there long enough to marry an attractive girl named Elizabeth Egan, and to bowl with distinction for the South Melbourne and Prahran

District Clubs. Fortunately for him, his second game for his State was against South Australia, and he collected wickets with such enthusiasm that an invitation to shift his quarters to Adelaide was quickly forthcoming. The rest of the Grimmett story became part of the history of Australian cricket.

Clarrie Grimmett was an adventurous customer, completely sold on the idea that he had the bowling ability to lead him on to fame and fortune. He accomplished the first objective without doubt, but the second always managed to elude him. As a young, certificated member of the sign-writing trade he had packed up his bags and left Auckland just before the First War began. He set out for Sydney, where he hoped to learn something from great men like M. A. Noble, then at the end of a magnificent international career as one of the greatest all-rounders the game had known. With Noble in his sights, Grimmett joined up with the Sydney Club, which was Noble's stamping ground. Quick, as always, on the uptake, he discovered that all the New South Wales cricket plenipotentiaries were completely entranced with the capabilities of Arthur Mailey, successor to H. V. Hordern. Prompted no doubt by Elizabeth Egan, whom he had met on a brief southern holiday, he decided a change of venue to Melbourne was necessary.

Mailey's bowling techniques never did appeal to Grum. Indeed in his quiet analytical way he was inclined to spurn the profligate attitude Arthur had to the presentation of easy runs to the opposition. The Mailey idea of concentrating almost entirely upon spin, to the detriment of both length and direction, filled Clarrie with horror. The two great bowlers had little in common. Mailey went about his business as if he knew that the batsmen supporting him were sure to knock off whatever runs were required of them for victory. Indeed he was often heard to congratulate, or seen to clap, an adventurous batsman who clouted one of his deliveries over the boundary fence. From the Sydney Hill one day I saw Mailey clean bowl Victorian Les Keating, an aggressive right-handed batsman, with a delivery which bounced twice before hitting the stumps. I distinctly remember Keating, nose knee-high, using his bat more in the way of a scythe as he tried unsuccessfully to deal with the second bounce. Mailey's philosophy allowed him to regard that delivery as a good ball – it got a wicket. Grimmett's reaction would have been contemptuous, as mine was, even though I was still in short pants and sitting on the Hill.

As the great cricket writer and music critic Neville Cardus said, 'Mailey bowled as a millionaire, Grimmett as a miser.'

Grimmett made his Test debut against A. E. R. Gilligan's side in 1924-25, and in his first Test, the fifth Test of the series, took 5 for 45 from 12 overs in the first innings and 6 for 37 from 19 overs in the second. Mailey was called on to bowl only 5 overs in the match, without success.

The two great spinners bowled in double harness in England in 1926, and were the mainstay of Australia's bowling. Grimmett bowled 204 overs in the Tests, for 13 wickets and 414 runs. Mailey bowled 172 overs for 14 wickets and 592 runs. By the Australian summer of 1928-29, Arthur Mailey had departed the Test cricket scene. Against Percy Chapman's team, Grimmett bowled 398 overs, almost twice as many as any other bowler, and took 23 wickets for 1024 runs. In England in 1930 he took 29 wickets for 925 runs from 350 overs. He took 33 wickets against the West Indies in 1930-31 and the same number against Jock Cameron's 1931-32 South Africans, and it was in that series, in the fourth and fifth Tests, that I became his bowling partner.

I watched him like a hawk, learning every trick of technique and temperament which he had to offer.

His policy was to keep each batsman strictly on his guard throughout his innings. He knew that his first deliveries to a batsman he had not bowled at before were paramountly important. His primary objective was to test his defence, especially on the back foot, and to initiate a probing campaign designed to tell him the innermost secrets of both defence and footwork in the shortest possible time. Grimmett knew that spinning the ball was a hopelessly inadequate skill unless it was allied with the strategically vital ability to lead the victim into a footwork indiscretion that would give spin the chance to play its vital part.

Time and again I heard Stan McCabe, batting carefully, say to him, 'Come on Grum, pitch one up.' Clarrie's response never altered. He smiled pleasantly and kept pushing the ball through to the very same spot from which McCabe knew that it was fatal to attempt to get down the track to try to drive. Absolute accuracy was his keynote. If early probing revealed a weakness on the leg stump, then that weakness would be attacked forthwith. Once he realized that a batsman was quick on his feet and anxious to get on with his driving, you could bet your place in the team that any driving that particular batsman would do would take place only when a rush of blood to the head encouraged him to 'have a go'. Walter Hammond, were he about today, could readily testify to the soundness of the Grimmett policy, and I assure you that Hammond was one of the greatest drivers that ever took bat in hand.

Grimmett lofted the ball high only when he was having fun with tailend batsmen, who quickly added to his wicket tally by opening their shoulders far too wide in showing what they could do to the world's best bowler. Those tailenders were the material on which Grum showed how masterfully he could spin his leg break, and to them his wrong 'un was so lethal that few were fully aware that it was merely a ball, not a handful of confetti that Grum had served up to them.

Grimmett's principles were mine too. In all my career I can remember bowling only one ball which I hoped would be swung powerfully to the leg side boundary, and that was delivered far away in the Scottish Highlands where I knew it would cause no difficulties for my cricket future. When the young student son of Lord Wigram, equerry to King George V who had thrilled us all with his Windsor Castle hospitality earlier in the 1934 tour, came to bat in the dying stages of the match Ramsay MacDonald had arranged at Forres on Moray Firth, I entertained him with the juiciest leg-side full toss imaginable, thereby I thought settling a debt of honour. Young Wigram smacked it gratefully for four, and then went on to top-score for Scotland.

Grimmett and I bowled together in perfect harmony, each with a careful eye on the other. With him at the other end I knew full well that no batsman would be allowed the slightest respite. We were fortunate in that our styles supplemented each other. Grum loved to bowl into the wind, which gave him the opportunity to use wind resistance as an important adjunct to his schemes regarding direction. He had no illusions about the ball 'dropping', as we so often hear these days, before its arrival at the batsman's proposed point of contact. To him that was balderdash. In fact he always loved to hear people making up verbal explanations for the suspected trickery that had brought about a batsman's downfall. If a batsman thought the ball had dropped, well and good. Grimmett himself knew that it was simply change of pace that had made the batsman think such an impossibility had happened. Yet we still hear people talking about dropping as if it were a fully accredited part of the slow bowling procedure. It is good, I suppose, for the knowledgeable slow bowlers still in existence that such prattle still goes on, but it must act as an awful deterrent to the boy who sets out to become a reliable spinner. 'How,' he will ask, 'do you make a ball drop?' I hope he never asks me.

Clarrie Grimmett's career met with an underserved check during the bodyline series, when he suffered the humiliation of being omitted from the Australian side for the last two Tests. I never did get to the bottom of that story, but I am quite certain that there was clandestine skulduggery going on, for I was as certain then as I am now that Grum was the best bowler in the world at the time. In the first Test England got an enormous score and we bowlers had a proper dressing down. In Melbourne, Tim Wall, Bert Ironmonger and I had taken all the wickets necessary to win the game quite handsomely. In Adelaide, the boil-over match, Australia lost pretty conclusively, but Grimmett bowled more than 60 overs there for 3 wickets in all and certainly did not let his team down.

Perhaps my own form had contributed to the feeling that Australia could do without Grimmett, allowing the selectors the chance to bolster the fading batting line-up. Bill Woodfull, our captain, had promoted me to the new ball bowling role in Melbourne, and had carried on with this idea in Adelaide. That of course meant that my job shifted over from swing to spin as soon as the seam began to flatten. My services therefore were in such demand that I was called upon to bowl 50 overs in each innings, whilst my esteemed partner took a relatively back seat.

Whatever the reason for his omission, you can take it from me that it was misguided and hopelessly wrong. He had bowled tight throughout, and although wickets had not come his way, he was still a top-liner. When I first heard that he had been dropped, I wondered whether the demented selectors had been overly impressed with Don Bradman's leg spinning form in England's second innings of the infamous Adelaide Test. In bowling his four overs of lofted leg breaks, Bradman had snared the prized wicket of Walter Hammond, who snicked a wide full toss into his stumps as he apparently tried to annihilate the Members' Stand just before the tea adjournment. Woodfull gave Bradman a further seven overs in England's first innings of the fourth Test, but that was Bradman's swan song as a slow bowler, apart from a few overs he had during England's mammoth innings in the final 1938 Test when he fell and sprained his ankle.

Undeterred by this selection humiliation and untroubled by the forty-two years which some people evidently thought were beginning to lie too heavily upon his bowling shoulder, Grimmett carried on in his usual determined fashion to gain a place in the Australian 1934 tour of England, where he played a crucially prominent part in regaining the Ashes.

It was on that tour that we had all the verbal bouquets in the cricket world thrown at us as one of the greatest spin combinations Test cricket had seen. Bowling tightly and keeping the batsmen unremittingly on the defensive, we collected 55 of the 73 English Test wickets that fell that summer. Each of us collected more than a hundred wickets on tour and it would have needed a brave, or demented, Australian at that time to suggest that Grimmett's career was almost ended.

At the end of the following year, 1935, with Bradman unavailable, Clarrie was probably the first man chosen to join the first full-scale tour to South Africa, under the captaincy of his South Australian mate Victor Richardson. I have already dealt with Grum's amazing performance in South Africa, where he took 44 wickets in Tests at an average of 14.59. Only two men, S. F. Barnes and J. C. Laker, have taken more wickets in a series.

And yet a year later he had been replaced in the Australian team by Frank Ward, who was to play in four Tests and take 11 wickets at an average of 52.18. Even today, the thought of his omission from the 1936-37 and 1938 series makes me boil with rage. How could the selectors have been so stupid?

Never has it entered my head that any batsman could possibly vie with Bradman for the laurel wreath fit for the world's best to wear on his brow. Exactly the same goes with me for Clarence Victor Grimmett, than whom no better bowler ever breathed. Their contributions to Australian cricket were inestimable.

As a final note, I would not want it to go unrecorded that towards the end of his illustrious career I was able to introduce Clarence Grimmett to the joys of a quiet beer or two in the dressing room after a day's play. Previously he had taken his bowling task so seriously as to necessitate a policy of abstinence. In later years he expressed to me on a number of occasions his regret at the pleasures he had missed early in his career, and it is a source of no little pride in me that I was able to help him overcome his earlier shortcomings.

STAN McCABE

To give credit where it's due, if the non-selection of Clarrie Grimmett was one of cricket's classic clangers, the choice of the young Stan McCabe to go to England in 1930, before he had scored a century in a Sheffield Shield match, was one of cricket's master strokes.

McCabe went to 'Joey's', St Joseph's College at Hunters Hill, where he won his way into the First XI and the First XV before he was sixteen years of age. Many thought that Stan should have taken full advantage of the bursary he had won as an eleven-year-old candidate from the Grenfell Convent School which entitled him to five years secondary tuition at St Joseph's, but Stanley decided he had had enough after negotiating the Intermediate Certificate, and went home to take up a job in a local accountancy office.

I met him first during the Easter period of 1927 when I was lucky enough, having been granted an extra week's holiday from school as a gracious governmental gesture to celebrate the visit of the Duke and Duchess of York, to travel with a team to Young over the Easter weekend.

How lucky we were to get away from Sydney where torrential rain fell throughout the Easter holiday period. It was so wet that the Royal Show was absolutely ruined and the mudlarks won all the important races at Randwick – and thereby hangs a tale. Sitting in a tram on the way home from work, I heard the tram driver discussing prospects for the races over the weekend. The conductor, a clued-up young man who wore his cap at just the right angle and talked knowingly through the corner of his mouth, offered the suggestion that if the heavy rain which the weather bureau was prophesying eventuated, then a horse called 'Don Moon' was home and hosed. He was, the conductor said, the only real mudlark in the race. His authority on the subject impressed me, who knew nothing whatever about racing, so strongly that I remembered what he had said, and when I reached Young the next day, having heard that the rain had started to pour down in Sydney, I told all the locals that I had the good oil from a very powerful source that 'Don Moon' was a certainty. It duly won, and my reputation was made in Young long before I got a cricket ball in my hands. Wisely I refrained from further efforts in that field.

Although I had travelled along with the Sydney team, I did not play for them. My brother Jack was working locally with the Department of Agriculture, and I had promised to play for the local team, with whom he played. This was a lucky break for me, because I was able to bowl against two influential Sydney cricketers in the touring team whom I had not met in the short time I had been playing in Sydney Grade cricket. One of them was Andrew Ratcliffe, the skipper of the Glebe District Cricket Club and a wicketkeeper-batsman of such skill that many good judges considered him unlucky not to have been chosen for the 1926 tour of England. Better still from my point of view, Ratcliffe happened to be a New South Wales selector. The other VIP was Edwin 'Chappie' Dwyer, captain of the Mosman Club, a former NSW Sheffield Shield batsman and a future NSW and Australian selector. As an Australian selector Chappie Dwyer had an attribute which was almost unique in my experience: he had a personal touch which appealed to everybody. He would often come along to talk to the players and get their opinions; he knew how, when, and where to give someone a pat on the back, and he was a good manager of men.

So the weekend was already, in my mind, a most important occasion.

I was a spectator when the touring team played the Grenfell Juniors on the second day of the holiday, and I was very deeply impressed with the startling ability of the local side, who were more or less all teenagers. Four members of the McCabe clan were in the Grenfell side. It was difficult to tell one from another, they looked so much alike, but two of them, Les and Stan, stood out like beacons on the cricket field. It was a concrete wicket and the canvas mat kept blowing up irritatingly in the strong westerly wind which blew across the flat where Henry Lawson had been born. Nevertheless the two enterprising young men batted so confidently that the Sydney attack paled into insignificance. I was quite glad to be a non-combatant, enjoying the comfort of the front seat of a Wolseley car.

When the match finished I repaired to one of the local pubs to lay the dust, and there I ran face to face with the younger McCabe. What a great place for us to meet! With his cricket boots tied together by their laces and slung over his left shoulder in typical schoolboy fashion, he had come to the hostelry with his mate Sep O'Loughlin to polish off a mug of squash on the way home. I knew Sep O'Loughlin, who introduced us, because he and I happened to have been school-mates at St Patrick's a few years before.

McCabe did not have long to blush unseen in country cricket. As soon as Chappie Dwyer was appointed to the Country Committee of the NSW Cricket Association he set about organizing the future of the talented young man who had batted so well against his team at Grenfell. The story goes that Dwyer was unsure which of the two McCabes, Stan or Les, most deserved an invitation to play in Sydney and that his nomination of Stan was a sort of blind man's buff operation. If it's true, then it was a most fortuitous piece of guesswork. Les McCabe undoubtedly was a top bracket country player, and he did get an invitation later, but it would need a most fertile imagination to believe that he had more ability than his young brother. Les himself always maintained that Dwyer had certainly pulled the right rein in naming Stan.

In three years that rosy-cheeked country boy with the infectious smile was chosen as a member of the young Australian side that Bill Woodfull was invited to lead on tour in England in 1930. From the time of his elevation to that arena McCabe never missed a Test until he retired from the game at the early age of 28, after having made three tours of England and one to South Africa, and having skippered NSW successfully for three seasons following the retirement of his close friend Alan Kippax.

McCabe was my batsman hero. Never did I willingly miss a moment of an innings from him even on the long tours of England where cricket often became a drudgery. I have already mentioned the three great innings he played. The first in Sydney in 1932 when he smashed Douglas Jardine's bodyline plan to pieces, the second in Johannesburg in 1935, the third at Trent Bridge, Nottingham, in 1938, when his contribution of 232 constituted more than half of Australia's first innings total in the first Test of that series. If I could organize my reincarnation as an international batsman, I would settle for a role identical with that which Stan McCabe encircled the hearts of spectators right round the cricket world.

Let me try to give a pen-picture of the points which made McCabe my batting hero.

He had great ball sense. He could shine at any game in which a ball played its part. He was a first-class player of billiards and snooker, with a finesse acquired from the childish days when he had to borrow a stool to practise his shots on the billiard table behind his father Bill's hairdressing salon in Grenfell's main street. Talking of which, it always seemed quite incongruous to me that Bill McCabe and each of his four sons were all as bald as the billiard balls aforesaid, while Bill earned his living from shearing the locks of his country clients. Stan, perhaps with a trick learned in his father's salon, was one of those rare mortals who, using the old fashioned cut-throat razor, having shaved half his face with his right hand, could complete the job with his left. It frightened me in watching.

His incomparable gift of timing enabled him to strike the ball in any direction at seemingly incredible speed. To watch him back cutting was the very essence of delight and admiration of the manner in which he transferred his weight from his left foot to his right at the precise moment required, to steer the ball through the slips field with the same dexterity he could pot a snooker ball. McCabe lived at a time when the late cut was looked upon as undeniable evidence of batting skill, and he completely mastered it.

As a new ball exponent in the bowling department, McCabe regarded himself as no more than an honest workhorse who could be counted on to back daily into the shafts and perform reliably. In this opinion he was supported by many of his team-mates, myself included. Many was the time that I tried to persuade Stan to drop his portfolio as a bowler, but such was his dedicated attitude to teamsmanship that he never listened to me. My idea was that he sacrificed the finest edge of his amazing batting capacities by involving himself in the savage demands that bowling made upon them. Keith Miller was another whom I tried strenuously to convince that he was much too good a batsman to squander such unusual talent in the rough and tumble of speed bowling.

The fact is, lest it be forgotten, that McCabe opened the bowling for Australia in a dozen or so of his 39 Tests and took 36 Test wickets at an average of 43. Because of his bowling activities McCabe was classed as a top-line all-rounder, a classification that always raised a slight blush. He used the old adage, 'Jack of all trades and master of none,' in sizing up his own cricket role, but in that view he found no support from his team-mates, none of whom had the slightest doubt about his claim to be regarded as a batsman of the very highest calibre.

Having spent a long apprenticeship in the sporting goods department of a large Sydney firm, he went into the trade on his own account on his return from the 1938 tour of England, opening a shop which still flourishes in Sydney's main thoroughfare, George Street. The business was going strongly at the time the Second

World War brought to a quick end Australia's concentrated involvement with sport.

Stan joined the army, although his friends knew this was but a fine patriotic gesture that never could lead to any prolonged involvement in the rough and tumble of army life. His feet, which had given him so much trouble throughout his cricket life, landed him a desk job at Sydney's Victoria Barracks. Few people knew that malformation of his feet almost caused McCabe to fail the medical examination for his place in Woodfull's 1930 touring team, his first overseas trip. When he stood barefooted before the medical officer, he had to answer many questions about balance, aching muscles, and bruised soles when critical notice was taken of his extraordinarily high insteps and the peculiar fact that when he stood at ease his toes did not touch the floor. Suspect from the start, his feet brought about the end of his illustrious career. Even if the Second World War had not taken place, it is certain that Stan McCabe would never again have been fit enough to undertake a demanding tour.

For the remainder of his life Stan's health declined disappointingly. Not long before his death I visited him in the Mater Misericordiae Hospital where he was being treated for a liver complaint, and was shattered to find him so weak. He died in a melancholy manner. At the back of his home the unfenced garden fell cliff-like into a tangled growth of gum trees and bush which made up the nature strip lying between his home and the water of Sydney's Middle Harbour at Beauty Point. When Chappie Dwyer visited one Sunday morning, to see Stan and his wife Edna after Stan's return from hospital, they noticed a dead possum which was lying on the back lawn apparently having handed in its chips at the end of a long innings. In the course of their conversation Stan said that he would go down later on and consign the body to the nature strip with a well-directed throw from the boundary, a programme which Dwyer was quick to discourage having noticed the frailty and uncertainty with which Stan was performing. That afternoon Stan's body was found at the bottom of the shallow cliff. He had despatched the possum as intended, but had gone overboard with it.

Stan McCabe was an ornament to the game of cricket. Never have I heard one word of harsh criticism aimed at him. He was everyone's esteemed friend, especially mine. I count it as one of the treasures of my life that I was privileged to spend so many years of my sporting life in his magnificent company.

England has good cause to idolize the memory of the 'kind and manly Alfred Mynn', their legendary cricketer from Kent. I feel certain that McCabe's name will take on a similar aura in Australia in the years that lie ahead. Australian cricket will forever be indebted to the beautiful little southwestern New South Wales town of Grenfell, which gave to it Stanley Joseph McCabe, a gentleman cricketer if ever one worthy of the term lived in this country.

BILL WOODFULL

Any tribute one might wish to pay to William Maldon Woodfull, arguably Australia's most uniquely successful cricket captain, must necessarily take into detailed examination the infamous bodyline tactics instigated and since banned by England. Woodfull steadfastly refused to reply in kind to Jardine's appalling attack on the bodies of every opposing Australian batsman worthy of its attention.

There was never a doubt in any Australian cricketer's mind that season that the type of attack used by our opposition was aimed primarily at frightening the wits out of every batsman who confronted it. To the devil with all the childish balderdash which went on around the tables so safely placed in a back room at Lord's, and in the high places which seem to have come so recently into the public ken. It never occurred to me that any sane person who knew what was going on could possibly have thought that it was not unsportsmanlike. I know that the use of that word made the whole thing blow up into the infamous episode which will never be forgotten, but it is a point to be conceded that the English administration choked on humble pie. Certainly they couldn't stomach that one word, and more is the pity, for them.

The argument galloped away from the cricket fields, where it should have been confined and resolved, and found itself swallowed up avidly in the political jargon that has the irritating ability to make thinking men laugh mirthlessly.

How many times have you had to listen to such tripe as: 'The Australians could never have retaliated on the field because they had no bowler fast enough to mount a similar campaign', or 'Larwood was so devastatingly accurate in his methods that Australia had no real capacity to return the bitter medicine'? What unmitigated nonsense! Such lines of thought originated in the minds of men who never got closer to a cricket field than the comfortable surrounds of a committee room table where free drinks are known to make the tongue wag loosely and the brain ossify.

No great accuracy is required to bash a ball down short enough to make it bounce head-high. You have to be accurate enough to keep the ball on a line that is certain to have it creating problems when it reaches its ultimate target, but that should come as second nature to any bowler in the international sphere.

Length! Who dares speak about it when bodyline bowling is being discussed. The village blacksmith could hurl the ball down indiscriminately satisfying all the demands that 'length' is likely to demand of him in that regard.

Larwood was a great bowler, but it is absolutely unacceptable to talk about Larwood's magnificent control of length and direction during that season. Length and direction had nothing whatever to do with his extraordinary success—success which had eluded him on his previous Australian tour in 1928-29 and against Australia in England in 1930.

Australians could have bowled exactly the same rubbish had 'Old Steadfast', our highly respected leader, decided to give it a go. There has always been a crop of vigorous young pace bowlers whose athleticism and enthusiasm could be directed to a bowling strategy that demands little more than a murderous glint in the eye and a facility for pitching the ball deliberately short. Even I, in a playful mood on the SCG one morning, bowling against Victorian right-handed opener Keith Rigg before a Sheffield Shield crowd of well over twenty thousand, dropped my quicky short and watched it remove Rigg's cap as he attempted to hook it. How would I have gone if I had been given six men packed close in on the leg side bowling my fast ball six times an over? I know I would have done better than the 27 wickets I got against that England side employing my normal bowling methods.

How would Tim Wall have gone? Or Bull Alexander? Eddie Gilbert, the Queensland Aborigine who could make skin and hair fly, would have made bouncer bowling to a packed leg side field a terrifying prospect for the majority of England's slow-footed batsmen. I am not prepared to listen to any talk whatever about Australia not being able to have retaliated in kind.

As I look back now through the crowded years of a long cricket life spent in the field and in the Press Boxes where I have watched with critical eyes the progress of the game through close on one hundred and fifty Tests, I cannot escape the feeling that the bodyline business might easily have been settled amongst the players–the ones who were so involved with and so infinitely aware of all its ramifications. Why was it not brought to a head like it would have been had it been a game of football? Why was physical force not shown in a sudden fit of temper? Why did Australian players remain docilely on the receiving end knowing full well that they were nothing better than the targets set up for a completely unsporting campaign? Never once did I hear an Englishman threatened. That fact mesmerizes me now as I think about it. Having watched the growing emphasis placed on the bouncer in modern Test cricket, and the wicket-capturing results obtained by this modern bowling tactic, which can fairly be regarded as cream-puff stuff compared with the real McCoy served up by Larwood and Voce, I wonder at the moderation of the healthy young Australians who took it all so uncomplainingly on the chin fifty years ago.

The present bouncer business has engendered widespread discontent throughout the cricket world. There have as well been many instances of flaring tempers highlighted by kicking, brandishing bats, the emergence of a new line of conduct known as 'sledging', kicking stumps out of the ground and the Lord alone knows what else.

Why in the bodyline summer did not some resourceful Australian, goaded beyond forbearance, resort to the age-old use of the knuckle? Many a difficult situation has been overcome and frayed tempers patched up completely and forever with a good old 'dust-up' in the confines of the dressing room.

The answer, and I am as certain of it as of the cosmic fact that night follows day, is that violence would have erupted mid-field during that disgraceful season had it not been for the magnificient character of the heroic William Maldon Woodfull, who led his team so bravely throughout that dreadful summer.

Bill Woodfull's outstanding personal courage was the keynote of the enormous contribution he made to Australian cricket during his inspiring leadership. As I look back now and see him picking himself up from the ground, I wonder whether I have ever seen a braver man. Felled by bowling which demanded nothing less than quintessential courage to take squarely on the body without squirming, I am sure that cricket in all its history never provided a more inspiring sight than that of Bill Woodfull resuming his painful stance at the wickets, prepared to resume the game, still determined to offer whatever sacrifice his noble dedication to his captaincy demanded of him. It was the stuff that Empires were made of.

Bodyline was a brutal campaign which would certainly have justified equally unacceptable reprisals, but Woodfull's glorious reaction to it so inspired me and my team-mates that it was possible for us to accept it. Woodfull knew, and through him we knew, that we were being called upon to make a colossal sacrifice for the good of the game. Had Woodfull not been an inspired leader, had he not so thoroughly earned our admiration, cricket could have been dealt such an agonizing blow that its continuance could have been lost forever. It was bad enough as it was, but imagine what would have happened had an Australian captain entered upon a policy of retaliation. See what you can make of the scene. Forget the nonsense that Australia could not have retaliated. That line of chatter is quite as silly as those who enter into it.

Bill Woodfull saved Australia from the disgrace that a wholesale bodyline war would have entailed had he deliberately turned those reprehensible bodyline tactics back on Jardine's team immediately after the opening of hostilities in the memorable first Test in

Sydney. His name will grow in stature as the years roll by. The significance of his 'no reprisals' policy will tend to add lustre to his name in the eyes of cricket enthusiasts right round the world.

As a closing shot I find it fitting to remind everyone concerned with the bodyline story that, having been felled by a bouncer from Larwood in the first innings, W. M. Woodfull batted right through the second innings of that ill-fated Adelaide Test. 'Old Steadfast' they all called him. You can shout it as loudly as you like, I'll still listen.

25 Cricket with a Typewriter

In 1939 I went to work in the office of the Lion Tile Company, at Enfield, at the insistence of Walter Tidmarsh, whose family were major shareholders.

Not long after, I undertook my physical examination to see what part I was to play in the War against Hitler. The old army doctor who measured my chest said, 'You'll get a trip for certain', but as I was beyond military age I imagined myself with a manual job in some obscure branch of the Australian armed forces. However the Department of War Organization then took a hand in the proceedings. The War was not expected to last long, and the Department classified Lion Tile as a protected undertaking, to be ready to resume full production as soon as the War ended. I was ordered to remain there, which I did for the next 36 years.

My active cricket life ended in 1946 when I returned from a lightning tour of New Zealand, in which we played five matches including the first ever official Test between our two countries.

That tour was again made memorable by the parsimonious attitude of the Board of Control. Twelve players only were invited to tour, at the princely stipend of £1 sterling per diem. Each player was supplied with a green and gold blazer with the three letters A, B and C emblazoned on the pocket. No one ever gave us an explanation for the logo, and it certainly had the New Zealanders nonplussed, although one Auckland schoolboy reckoned that it must have stood for 'Australia's Best Cricketers'.

New Zealand enthusiasts turned up in such force that an official approach was made to our Board by the New Zealand Board to increase the daily pay of our team members as a gesture of appreciation. The Australian Board generously refused. This miserly attitude amazed the members of that young team, most of whom had just been demobilized – four of them indeed were still wearing uniforms.

A recurrence of my left knee trouble worried me throughout the short tour, and so I decided that the time had come to close my long innings. Returning to our dressing room after we had successfully terminated our commitments with a Test victory at Wellington, I removed my cricket boots and threw them through the window as a gesture of complete surrender.

A few months later, with the revival of international cricket between England and Australia in the offing, I began to receive interesting propositions from Australian and English newspapers to write on the coming 1946 series of Tests between the two countries.

The *Sydney Morning Herald* invited me to call to be interviewed by their Mr Angus McLachlan with a writing contract in view. I accepted Mr McLachlan's terms and settled down comfortably to a pleasant relationship which has gone on smoothly to the present day. So smoothly indeed that I have worked in harmony with a succession of top line executives of that great daily whom I have never seen. I doubt if the sum total of my visits to the 'office' has yet reached double figures.

With this arrangement resolved and publicized, the London *Daily Express* soon offered terms which attracted me. It was then that the Melbourne businessman Mr John Wren wrote to make me an offer to ensure I would play for Australia against England in the approaching series. He offered to pay me the sum total of my newspaper contracts if I agreed to play cricket. It was certainly generous, but I had to inform him that there was no hope for me to play, as I was physically not fit.

Then began for me a wonderful working association with my friend Tom Goodman, to whom I have often gratefully expressed my deep appreciation for the enormous influence he had upon my falling into line as a cricket writer. It seems like undervaluing him to say that he was the most dedicated person with whom I have ever worked. Tom was on duty twenty-four hours a day on tour if the situation demanded his constant attention. I am prepared to bet that he never missed a point of interest, and that at a time when there were no press handouts from the Board or the dressing room as there are today.

His high standard of ethics was so well known throughout the whole cricket world that he was designated as a complete 'trusty' by administrators and players alike. If some piece of hot news was branded 'background music only', Tom was one of the very few who would ever get wind of it, and he knew exactly what to do with it. There is no doubt that I was lucky to start under Tom Goodman's professional wing, and I quickly realized that my course had to be set entirely upon what happened out in the field of play, where my many years of active involvement gave my opinion some weight. Tom had every other feature well and truly covered.

So it was that I decided, from the very first day that I took up my pen, that I would never knock upon or even wish to enter a dressing room door with the hope of an inside story. My policy was always to rely entirely upon my own long experience and to write exactly what I thought in the most forthright manner possible. That has remained my style throughout, and it has suited me very well. The Australian captain in my first series, Bill Woodfull, allowed no visitor at any time into the team's dressing room. A clear memory remains with me of Woodfull asking a member of the Australian Board of Control who had presumptuously entered for some urgent discussion, to leave the room and to wait for the captain's formal invitation through the official door-keeper. In fact I have often wondered how Plum Warner got past the Adelaide door-keeper to deliver his famous apology during the third Test in 1933.

Many times the opportunity has come to give my own personal opinions upon matters of great controversy. One of these arrived on the scene in the very first Test match I covered; it was the 'Bradman caught Ikin' incident at Brisbane in 1946. From the

'Gabba Press Box, then situated out on the horizon at wide mid-on, I unhesitatingly ruled against the batsman. Bradman, ill at ease against a much slower Bill Voce, sent the ball, a half-volley, so quickly to Jack Ikin fielding fine of gully slip that it spun the fieldsman round as he took the ball two-handed at the point of his right shoulder. Bradman stayed put, so I assumed the Australian skipper thought that he had hit the ball into the ground.

But in my book he was out, and along with thousands of others, I said so. Significantly, two who didn't were my good friends Lindsay Hassett – Bradman's batting partner at the time – and George Borwick, the umpire.

Press Boxes are not always the best places to get a first-class view of what goes on. Some are shockers. The worst in Australia is at Adelaide, which is side-on to the pitch. It is the only Australian Test match ground where the press sit square on to proceedings, and Adelaide is the place where most of the interpretation troubles originate so far as the press writers are concerned. Should you want a few examples I will mention the exit of Oldfield per medium of a whack on the head in the third Test in 1933. Oldfield snicked that one onto his temple as he tried to hook, but it was reported as a direct hit. In later times the debate over Ray Lindwall's long drag in the final delivery stride came to a rowdy climax when the English press had such a wonderful view of it in 1946. And when Gordon Rorke's similar yet much longer drag came to light several years later it served to change the no ball rule to the ridiculous regulation which now exists. Side-on Press Boxes should be abolished.

It is a funny thing that the best viewing positions at Adelaide's ground, renowned for its scenic backgrounds, are occupied by the bleachers. Perhaps its erstwhile preoccupation with Australian Rules Football caused the rush of blood to the original architect's head. Brisbane and Melbourne now have ideal viewing spots for the men who try to write knowingly, and Sydney is excellent if one can recover sufficiently to avail oneself of its privileges after scaling the ninety-two steps involved in reaching it.

I ran into a little press luncheon table 'shindy' in my first English

Test at Nottingham in 1948, when I expressed the opinion that Norman Yardley, England's youthful captain, had erred in allowing Bradman the advantage of a fielding substitute for Lindwall when England, in difficulties, batted the second time. I thought it good sportmanship entirely overdone, and said so.

The facts were that a splendid eighth wicket partnership between Hassett, who scored 137, and Lindwall, 42, had placed Australia in an almost unbeatable position. They had run well between wickets throughout, yet Neil Harvey, Australia's twelfth man and our best fieldsman, was allowed to substitute in the field for Lindwall a short time after the partnership ended. At lunch the next day a leading English cricket writer saw fit to call me to task, having read my comments in that morning's *Daily Express.* My Australian colleagues said that I won the contest on points.

Later in that same game the crowd took to Keith Miller and gave him a tremendous burst of larry-dooley for bouncing a few at Cyril Washbrook. Nottingham had not forgotten the reception given to its heroes Larwood and Voce in Australia sixteen years before. It was an easy matter for me, having played in all five bodyline Tests, to draw comparisons for my Australian and English readers. I decided that Miller's display, minus the packed leg field, was kid's stuff in comparison, to the great displeasure of the English press and public.

Bradman's 'blob' in his final Test at the Oval was considered an historic event, and I was an observer of that too. He had performed in his accustomed prolific style throughout the tour, and was given the usual deafening reception as he took his slow walk to the wicket. Responding to Yardley's call, the English team, caps doffed, surrounded The Don and gave three hearty British cheers to mark his farewell appearance. I was quite sure that the bowlers cheered louder and longer than the rest.

Taking block to Eric Hollies, a leg spinner who must have been shaking at the knees at the enormity of his task, Bradman dealt with the first ball safely enough. Then he fell for a perfect wrong 'un. The ball came back to beat the half-forward bat and hit the off stump. Bradman pulled off his gloves, tucked his bat under his left arm, and departed. The mesmerized London crowd were utterly speechless. Old Charlie Fry–England's former captain, Oxford triple blue, and world-class athlete–from his Press Box vantage point described the silence as 'blasphemous'. Finally the crowd recovered their voices and their vote of acclamation, first for Birmingham's white-haired boy Eric Hollies, and then for the departing Bradman, reached a decibel rating which I have not heard equalled.

My most difficult writing assignment occurred in Manchester in 1956 when England's off spinner Jim Laker collected the record bag of nineteen wickets at Old Trafford.

England, batting first, got away to a great start with Richardson, Cowdrey and Sheppard getting good scores before the fun began. For the first two sessions of the day the Australian attack fared hopelessly. The pitch was as dead as mutton and I had visions of another match like the final Oval Test in 1938, where I said the pitch had been laid out by an undertaker. But when Richie Benaud, bowling to England's captain Peter May, had him caught by Ron Archer fielding wide at gully slip, I sat bolt upright to take notice. The way that ball behaved suggested to me that the pitch had woken up and was about to turn on an exhibition of incredible partisanship. From that ball, late on the first day, the series became a joke. At the start of that fourth Test the result was square–one Test all. Australia were never again in the event from the moment that Archer took that unlikely catch.

Some of us had been alerted to expect trouble. George Duckworth, talking to Arthur Morris, Lindsay Hassett and me at the Patton Arms Hotel at Warrington, gave me such a peculiar answer to an amiable question about the wicket being prepared for the next day at Old Trafford that I was impelled to ask more. In effect Ducky assured us that it was going to be a 'turner' and that it might last two days. It did not last one.

Jim Laker could have knocked Australia over with his left arm if needs be on that pitch, and Old Trafford's groundsman had a lot of Australian brickbats thrown at him during and after the match, but George Duckworth and several Lancashire executives told us after the game was over that their groundsman had done exactly what he was told.

'Who told him?' was the pertinent question which Hassett asked, and 'Oh, Lindsay! You know very well who it was,' came the stern reply. That was a cooked wicket if ever I saw one. Good luck to Jim Laker, whose performance on it was impeccable, but the Australians were never in the race.

In all those years of cricket writing I have had a wonderful chance to keep up not only a close association with the game I have loved but also with the host of magnificent friends I have made and valued highly in many countries. But there have been one or two bad times that have detracted from the allure.

When, one Melbourne afternoon, I saw the stumps kicked down in a display of pique, I must admit that my stomach turned over. That preliminary blow to my preconceived opinion that cricket is the best game of them all conditioned me for the display of semi-armed combat where a bowler, with his boot, took on an opponent armed with a bat. I thought, that day in Perth, that the time I had been predicting, when undisciplined middle of the field behaviour would lead to an inevitable show of fisticuffs, had arrived. But the quick thinking of umpire Tony Crafter, who stepped bravely between the combatants, prevented it, thank God.

Sitting in Press Boxes around the world I have been lucky enough to see many important careers commence, and close. Harvey, Lindwall, Morris, Miller, O'Neill, the two Chappells, Walters, Benaud, Lawry, Simpson, Redpath, McKenzie, Grout, Marsh, Davidson and McDonald are the names of some of the Australians who made their entrances and their exits under my critical eye.

I have seen too the extraordinary and vigorous growth of the public entertainment known as limited-overs cricket, and have steadfastly refused to accept it as a serious substitute for the game which I have loved so much that I feel that I have some sort of proprietorial right to it. So long as limited-overs cricket is classed only as quick-fire public entertainment I am prepared to live alongside it, but I am appalled at the degenerating influence of the one-day game on the game as a whole.

Firstly, because there is no premium on taking wickets, limited-overs cricket is loaded against spin bowling and in favour of short pitched defensive bowling, which is of itself unattractive, and what is worse makes for unattractive batting. Batsmen will never learn to use their feet to bowling of this type, and will come to rely more and more on short-armed, clubbed strokes. The graceful off-side play of the Hammonds and Greg Chappells will disappear, and the game will come to resemble baseball.

It is only by encouraging spin bowling that footwork will be brought back into the game, and when I think that this new type of cricket is still played under the leg-before-wicket rules which have already gone a long way towards destroying the art of spin bowling, my bile rises to a level which is difficult for me to bear. Don't the administrators understand this? If not, how can they be so stupid?

The least they could do is give spinners a fair chance in the one-day game. That would be a golden opportunity to re-introduce a fair lbw rule, so that if a batsman is hit on the pad by a ball which would have hit the wicket, regardless of where it pitched, he is given out. Morally he is out. He should be given out. Limited-overs cricket would be a perfect place to experiment with such a rule, and it would have the enormous advantage of bringing spin bowling into the new game on equal and fair terms.

I am convinced too that the excess of cricket, particularly limited-overs cricket, played in England at the moment is the reason why the home of the game can no longer produce fast bowlers. The emphasis is on bowling tight, not on taking wickets, and with so much cricket being played any genuine tearaway would burn himself out in no time. The West Indian pace battery might seem to give the lie to this argument, but at present their nursery is much less intense – they arrive on the international scene fully formed, so to speak. If they start to take cricket too seriously in the West Indies, and overload the local game with coaches and too much cricket, my bet is that they will before too long run into the same problems.

One-day cricket is said to have brought the crowds back to the game. My attitude to that has always been that the game is for the players, the people inside the fence, not those outside it. But if crowds are essential for the well-being of the game, then my guess is that nothing will encourage them to watch the game more than classical cricket where both batsman and bowler are encouraged to play attacking cricket on equal terms. The biggest crowds I ever experienced in my playing days were in the 1936-37 series. That series was accompanied by very little controversy inside the fence, just glorious attacking cricket: the likes of Walter Hammond, Maurice Leyland, Gubby Allen and Hedley Verity for England, and Don Bradman, Stan McCabe, Ernie McCormick and Fleetwood-Smith and O'Reilly for us. It is interesting to note also that the other series out here which consistently drew enormous crowds was in 1960-61 against Frank Worrell's West Indies, when the same brand of cricket was played, perhaps for the last time. Even more interesting to me, that 1960-61 series was not dominated by fast bowling: Lance Gibbs and Richie Benaud played crucial roles in every nail-biting encounter.

I know how glorious the game can be. To me, limited-overs cricket is a travesty of the game, and I am certain that it is creating greater problems for the game in the long term than it is solving in the short term.

26 'Tiger'

Cricket is a wonderful vehicle for the expression of character and no phase of it is more powerful in that direction than the privilege of getting your hands on the ball to start a bowling session. To me bowling was the very essence of the game of cricket.

Such justification as there may be for my nickname was not earned from my efforts as a batsman. No one knew my batting limitations better than I, though Bill Woodfull might have had an inkling of the truth when he advised me on how to play Larwood: 'Don't get hit,' he said. He needn't have wasted his breath, really, because getting hit was certainly not something I was planning, although I was a bit less certain on how to go about it. In any case I would have been universally deemed to be unworthy of the extra effort required to frighten the daylights out of me, before despatching me to the pavilion per medium of a straight yorker. Come to think of it, perhaps it is a blot on them – perhaps my pride should be offended. In that extraordinary summer, overall campaign efficiency might have decreed that Larwood or Voce should try to wing me somewhere about the right shoulder to reduce my nuisance value as a member of the Australian bowling attack. But they would have had to be quick indeed to do that. I ran so hurriedly from the danger zone that it would have probably needed a well-planned wide to collide with me in my hasty retreats towards the square leg umpire.

I have admitted to the impatience which may have cost us the Lord's Test in 1934, when I tried to swat Verity out of that famous ground and so deprived myself of the chance to bowl on the worst wicket ever I saw in England. But I have also mentioned with pride my score of 37 not out – top score for Australia in the first innings in Sydney in 1936 – and there were other occasions on which I was able to swagger back into the dressing room preening my feathers, probably much to the amusement of the Bradmans and McCabes of this world who no doubt classed runs from the O'Reilly willow in the same category as hens' teeth.

For instance when I got 42 runs at Lord's in 1938 in partnership with my mate Bill Brown, who batted right through for 206 to become the first Australian ever to score two Test centuries at the famous London headquarters of the game, I was prepared only to speak by appointment with the lesser skilled men of my team like Donald Bradman (18) and Stanley McCabe (38).

There are two other occasions on which I will dwell in an effort to construct a solid argument in my defence. The first – which I make no apology for having mentioned previously – was at Old Trafford in 1934 when Australia was struggling desperately to save a follow on in chasing England's mammoth score of 627. During the course of the game several important members of our team were struck down with a throat infection which had first come to public notice when it laid low several leading tennis players then currently battling their way through the championships at Wimbledon. It was dubbed 'Wimbledon throat'. Bill Ponsford, Don Bradman and Arthur Chipperfield were three of the Test eleven who were declared 'hors de combat' after the game was well under way. Ponsford, opening the Australian innings with Bill Brown, had scored 12 when he fell victim to Walter Hammond's medium paced off breaks – a fact which even now my mate Bill would probably blushingly explain by saying that the 'wog' had already begun its devastating job. Bradman too fell to Hammond for 30. I was joined by my fast bowling friend Tim Wall when 9 Australian wickets were down for 454, still 24 runs short of saving the follow on. We took the score to 491, thus, in case you have missed the point, forcing England to bat again and giving the infected members of our team a chance to recover. The match was drawn.

And I would not want you to be ignorant of the fact that in my very first Test, the fourth Test against the South Africans in 1931-32, I figured in a record ninth wicket partnership. Only under pressure, when that performance comes up for discussion, do I reluctantly reveal that my partner was Don Bradman who finished with 299 not out, and that my contribution was 23. Yet it was quite a performance. My speed in running between the wickets was given full scope by my famous partner who strangely enough had so little confidence in me that he farmed the strike incessantly. Finally I failed to make the distance in time and the stumps were scattered by a throw from mid-on.

On the subject of South Africa, I know that my close friend Ernie McCormick, quick bowler and prince of popular touring companions, would never forgive me if I failed to recall the occasion when he and I sailed into the South African Test attack at the old Wanderers Ground in Johannesburg in 1936, and gave ourselves an opportunity to recount stories of our derring-do on the many occasions which we ourselves consider to be appropriate. My 56 not out then was my highest Test score.

During one of the early games of that tour, against Transvaal, a couple of the local batsmen – Buster Nupen and Chud Langton – took to Grimmett and me and hit a few sixes. They were good belts, too, right out of the ground, and they had to keep throwing replacement balls in. I was the first to suffer, much to Grimmett's delight, but then Chud hit him straight back over his head and over the railway line a couple of times, which took the sheen off his crockery. Finally, after yet another six clean out of the ground, Ernie McCormick, who like Stan McCabe was partial to a game of snooker, sauntered across to Vic Richardson and said in a stage-whisper, 'That's the end of the reds. Now we can get on with the coloureds.' Most of the blokes thought it was very funny at the time, although I didn't find the situation amusing. I took my bowling seriously.

As I have said, bowling was the essence of the game so far as I was concerned. Ball in hand, I was prepared to go on the warpath in search of batting prey, and I rejoiced in the battles, whether won or lost, along the track.

The main principles upon which I relied were direction and length: all things else were of comparatively little account.

When, in England in 1953, Richie Benaud came to me and asked to have a yarn about spin bowling, my advice to him could not have been simpler. I knew that he could bowl every variety of ball in the slow bowler's quiver, but I impressed on him the fact that he must get his basic leg break mechanically perfect, that variety came later, and should be used to emphasize the perfection of his stock-in-trade. I'm sure he did that, because later on, when his reputation was made, he freely acknowledged the help I had given him.

The ability to bowl consistently straight at the stumps is of prime importance. It is so basic to a bowler's technique that it is of 'sink or swim' proportions, and it is an easy virtue to develop and control. Constant practice provides it: not the constant practice associated with experience in matches or at the nets, but from the thousands of opportunities a boy with bowling in his blood gets as he bowls his way through his school days. An ambitious boy will arrange all his own opportunities to make himself bowl straight. The boy who is not interested enough to go carefully through this early stage would be well advised to forget altogether about a successful career in bowling. He would be better off cutting the lawn.

With direction more or less perfected the meaning of the term 'length' becomes absorbingly important. The best way to understand this is to become a highly observant batsman-watcher, taking special pains to notice the important difference between back foot defence and front foot defence.

When a batsman moves forward to a delivery, he invariably intends to meet it on the half-volley, where the ball contacts the surface of the pitch. When the ball is too short pitched for the bat to reach it on the half-volley, the batsman employs the back foot position. The successful slowish bowler tries to keep the batsman coming forward to him, the fast bowler prefers to have him on the back foot.

The reason for these preferred movements is so apparent that a thoughtful young bowler of ability never needs to have them explained. Suffice it to say that the bowler whose ambition is to do something off the pitch, as the slowish bowler does, banks all on the bat being offered at the half-volley point of contact.

If a bowler is good enought to detect the exact area of the pitch–the blind spot–where his opponent appears to be hesitant about committing himself confidently to either one of the defence positions, then he understands the meaning of the term 'length'.

He must remember that length is a variable area on the pitch. To a short batsman it is much further up the pitch than it is to a taller man who can reach further down. As a result a ball that would be on a good length to a tall batsman could easily be hooked to the leg side by a shorter one. This explains why it is so vitally important that a rising young bowler must not only be accurately consistent in bowling 'straight, to a length' but just as importantly he must learn to watch the batsman closely, to determine where that blind spot is situated for each particular batsman who arrives at the crease.

By far the most important trick of the bowling trade for the slowish bowler is his ability to effectively disguise his pace. I never became aware of a recipe for this that could be spelled out to a promising young bowler: I am quite sure there is not one. You can talk confusedly about a tight or a loose grip on the ball at the point of delivery, but the term 'change of pace' is so abstruse that it is likely to be regarded more or less as sleight of hand.

Here again ambition will force a bowler to learn from observing the tactics of a successful operator in the field. Don't ask to be told what to do, just watch that bowler with the utmost concentration and try to make up your mind what allows him to make the ball 'skid' through as if it came off a surface of ice, or what it was that created the impression that the ball 'dropped' suddenly before it reached the point of contact. Once a young bowler is aware of the tricks that can be manipulated he should retreat to his hideaway and make his own life practically unbearable by such consistent, never-ending practice that the tricks of the trade eventually open all their secret doors to him.

It is good, essential perhaps, to know from the start that no bowler ever could make the ball 'drop' or 'skid'. They are just familiar terms invented by bewildered batsmen to explain their shortcomings, or for cricket writers to show their familiarity with difficult phases of the bowling art. The term 'drop' comes of course from a batsman's failure to recognize the slower ball. 'Skid' comes from failing to spot the signs which tell that the faster ball is on its way. There is no need for an ambitious young man to be frightened by these terms. Once he has trained himself to bowl with consistent control of length he will be surprised by the ease with which the average batsman can be lured into danger.

A term which has become increasingly fatal in the slow bowling arena is described by the words 'loop' or 'looping'. My advice to the talented tyro is to shun these words as if they were germ-laden. So often one hears them bandied about that one tries hard to assess the woeful damage they have caused in the bowling department. To me they are anathema. The young bowler who thinks that he must toss the ball high in the air to satisfy his claims for recognition as a promising spinner is a fool. Tossing the ball high should be regarded as an unfailing sign that the bowler is wasting everybody's time, and would be much better off if he turned his attention to batting, or feeding the chooks.

I have seen looping bowlers never given the chance to hit the pitch when bowling to a quick-footed batsman free from the embarrassment of not knowing whether to go forward or back. A quick-footed batsman will always crucify a looping slow bowler. The best slow bowler ever, Clarrie Grimmett, never looped the ball when he was bowling boots and all. He would skip through on his short run and bring his arm over in a low trajectory aimed invariably at the middle and off stumps, forcing the batsman to play forward defensively.

If ever Grum descended to the world of fantasy by indulging in a little bit of looping, it was done only when he wished to have a bit of fun in making tailenders look foolish. I have even known him to keep such batsmen purposely at the wickets so that he could give his spinning repertoire a full airing, but it is impossible to bring to mind one occasion on which he looped a ball to quick-footed batsmen like Bradman, Hammond or McCabe. To them he came straight down the line, relying entirely upon his outstanding control of pace.

The grip is another topic I shall treat warily. There is no correct grip. An enthusiastic boy should get that into his head from the very start.

It is ludicrous to go to a coach and say, 'Please show me the correct grip for a leg break.' It is even more ridiculous for a coach to try to oblige. The correct grip is the grip which a bowler finds is correct for him. There is no universal correctness for gripping the ball. To elucidate that remark it is pertinent to say that Charlie Turner and I, the two Australian spinners who collected one hundred English Test wickets in less than twenty matches, were both told at our first appearance at city net practice that our grips were wrong and should be altered. Turner as an old man, long retired, was present at the Sydney nets when Arthur Mailey told me to change, and he won my deep affection by taking the trouble to sidle up and congratulate me on hearing me say, 'Thank you Mr Mailey for your interest, but I have been gripping like this since I was a small boy, and I guess I'll have to sink or swim by it now.'

Turner, 'The Terror', told me that he had had exactly the same experience when he came down from Bathurst to start his brilliant off spinning career in the 1880s.

My advice to a youngster is to grip the ball comfortably and make the ball revolve quickly as it leaves the hand. That is enough to know. The grip will be resolved personally as the young bowler comes to terms with his important job of making the ball revolve.

Another thing that cannot be coached, because it comes with the nature of the beast, is the intangible asset of temperament. Little can be done about it, for it was decided upon, I should think, at the moment of birth. It is the one quality which sets top line bowlers apart. Young bowlers on the way to the top are often discouraged from showing signs of temperamental behaviour. It is regarded almost always as a serious defect in a bowler's armoury if it becomes general knowledge that he can be induced to 'do his block'.

That, however, is not my interpretation of the real meaning of 'temperament', it smacks more of the seriously handicapping frailty once known as 'flashness'. To me, 'temperament' means the native ability to accept a challenge; the innate desire to emerge successfully from it; the self-control to behave calmly in the toughest situation; the drive to carry on doggedly when the going appears to be impossibly hard; the inbuilt urge never, never, never to accept defeat.

These probably will always remain unattainable, but no young bowler intent on success in the top bracket should ever cease trying.

In a recent article in the London *Observer* I noticed that Sir Leonard Hutton, writing of his record 364 runs in the 1938 Oval Test, paid me a compliment or two about persistent pugnacity in my 85-overs-long stint against him in that interminable engagement. However he took some of the wind out of my sails when he wrote that his fellow Yorkshireman, the likeable left-handed batsman Maurice Leyland, who contributed substantially in a long partnership with Hutton, said at one stage of the innings, 'One thing is certain: I have Tiger O'Reilly taped, and what's more he knows it.'

Maurice Leyland might have said it, but I am sure that he could not possibly have meant it. After Walter Hammond, whom I dismissed twelve times in Tests, Maurice was my next rabbit on the line. I landed his wicket ten times. I couldn't get him out that day, on that wicket, but Maurice never had me taped, and he knew it. He knew I never gave up.

If I have managed here to get the message across that a talented young bowler, bound for the top, should condition himself to do all his own thinking, and should cultivate an air of absolute self-confidence in confronting every batsman who crosses his path, I have accomplished what I set out to do. That's what I did. That's why they called me 'Tiger'.